FLOWER IN THE RIVER

NATALIE ZETT

NZ

N ZETT

Published by Zidova Publishing

Cover image: Steve Kocevar

Cover design: MiblArt

Editoral Consultant: Jay Blotcher

Book Coaching & Editorial Services: Ellie Stevenson

ISBN 978-1-7375796-1-8

www.flowerintheriver.com

Dedicated to the 844 who died on July 24, 1915

Memory Eternal

INTRODUCTION

While this is a work of historical fiction, the story is based on an actual event—the *Eastland* Disaster of 1915—which occurred in downtown Chicago. The *SS Eastland* was one of five ships chartered by Western Electric for its annual company picnic. The plan was to cross Lake Michigan and spend the day in Michigan City, Indiana.

About 2,570 people were aboard the *Eastland* when she capsized, while still moored in the Chicago River—844 were killed. Entire families, as well as many single young men and women, lost their lives.

"Within two minutes after it listed 45 degrees to port, it rolled over like a dead jungle monster shot through the heart," said Carl Sandburg, reporting for the *International Socialist Review*. 1

The *Eastland* Disaster was either ignored, forgotten, or buried for years—depending on who you talked to. In fact, many native Chicagoans grew up not knowing what occurred on July 24, 1915.

Just three years earlier, the RMS *Titanic* struck an iceberg, and was sunk in the North Atlantic Ocean. Yet, unlike the *Eastland*, the *Titanic* has managed to stay front and center in people's consciousness for over 100 years. One writer speculated that the *Titanic* passengers were "important people," whereas the immigrants, and children of immigrants, aboard the *Eastland* were not deemed significant. Another writer conjectured that the lives lost on the *Eastland* were of no significance, except to their families.

Flower in the River is a layered story of past and present; it's a tale where the ripples from a young woman's death are sensed by her grandniece decades after the tragedy.

When the grandniece receives a document that unlocks the buried secrets of her family's misfortunes, her life is thrown into a tailspin. She must do something, but what?

A vast, multigenerational account, set mainly in 1900s Chicago—and, later, in 1990s Minnesota—*Flower in the River,* follows the story of an Eastern European immigrant family who comes to the United States in the late 1890s. As with all immigrants, they hope for a better life, but, instead, are met with tragedy after tragedy.

Natalie Zett
Saint Paul, Minnesota

1

A FAMILY TALE UNTOLD

Stories may remain untold, but they are hardly lost, only misplaced for a time. The blood travels like a river through the body, and it remembers. It always remembers.

—from the journal of Zara Vrabel

Early Evening at the Pfeiffer House

July 24, 1915

Late afternoon dissolved into early evening as they gathered in the family parlor. Some sat on the dark mahogany dining room chairs, while others stood motionless, gazing at the frayed Oriental rug, fixating on its black and red squares and triangles.

Each carefully avoided the others' eyes. No contact could be made, for then reality would swallow them whole, and each would resent—or even hate—the other for merely not being her. Only the monotonous tick-tock of the grandfather clock proclaimed the truth: she had gone on, dancing over time's vast chasm, leaving them behind.

Stillness wafted over the Pfeiffer household for the first time.

With seven children, various aunts and uncles, and an endless stream of neighbors, the house had never known quiet until that day.

The Pfeiffer children heard it first from neighbors, who heard it from other neighbors who heard the newsies screaming in the streets. What they heard was some version of this story:

Picnic ship capsized in the river with people aboard!!

The Pfeiffer Household: earlier times

All the Pfeiffer children, even grown and married ones, remained close to the southwest Chicago abode, meandering in and out of the home, and one another's lives.

One afternoon, ten-year-old Eddie and fourteen-year-old Herman Junior, the only boys in the family, sat in the parlor playing cards. Twenty-two-year-old Annie and sixteen-year-old Martha were making stew in the kitchen when a loud shriek reverberated through the house, followed by screams and curses. Running to the parlor, Annie and Martha saw their brothers giggling and jabbing at each other. They heard a clip-thud, clip-thud, clip-thud as another sister, Louisa, descended the stairs, one shoe on and the other shoe dangling in her right hand. Tears streamed down her reddened, swollen face.

"What's wrong, Weesa? Forget how to put your shoes on?" said Annie.

"Shut up, wisenheimer! Oooh!!" screamed Louisa, hurling the shoe. "Look inside my shoe to see what she put there!"

Herman, slender, with a shock of red hair and freckles, picked the fancy high-button boot from the floor. He looked inside, extracted a wilted amphibian, and said, "How'd a dead frog get inside your shoe?"

"Climbed in there to get warm, and the smell probably killed it," said Annie, laughing. Herman and Eddie continued giggling.

"You all know how it got in there! Marrrrtha!!" screamed Louisa.

Martha smiled and shrugged her shoulders.

Seventeen-year-old Louisa should have been the chosen "pretty one" of the five sisters, with her hazel eyes, creamy porcelain skin, long, braided blond hair, and slender figure. Yet, Louisa's alternating histrionics and hypochondria superseded her beauty—and egged on her siblings, who devised small-scale tortures to wind her up. Hearing Louisa's cries from next door, their mother, Bertha, and Mrs. Thiele, a neighbor, raced to the Pfeiffer house to see Louisa crumpled on the floor whimpering.

Bertha sighed, closed her eyes, and shook her head. At 46, Bertha Straszynska Pfeiffer's blonde braids showed no hint of gray, and her clear, unlined, round face hinted at the beauty she once was.

"*Was ist das los?*" said Bertha, leaning over the sobbing Louisa.

"Oh, Louisa found a frog in her shoe," explained Herman, now joined by Martha.

When Mrs. Thiele saw the other children giggling as Bertha consoled her weeping offspring, she locked eyes with the culprit— Martha—and declared, "*Kinder,* they should be seen *und nicht* trouble *gemachen und nicht* noise *gemachen.*"

Bertha nodded to Mrs. Thiele and ushered her outside, where they remained in the gangway between their two homes, engaging in a spirited argument about child-rearing.

Mrs. Thiele never forgave Martha for trouncing her son, Johann. Martha was eight at the time, while Johann was a corpulent twelve-year-old.

"He deserved it, the fat bully," said Martha when Mrs. Thiele confronted the small, wiry girl about her son's black eye and bloody nose.

"Well, see how you like this," said Mrs. Thiele, slapping Martha's face.

Martha clenched her fist, ready to strike back when Herman intercepted, apologized to Mrs. Thiele, and took Martha back home. Martha glared at Herman and said, "Why did *you* apologize? Fat Johann started it!"

Remembering the event afresh, Martha tore past Louisa, flying up the stairs to the attic bedroom she shared with Louisa, Ida, and Eddie. Martha deliberately did not swallow for a minute or two. Opening the window, she saw her mother and Mrs. Thiele standing below.

Ready! Aim! fire! thought Martha, while spewing a huge spit wad downwards. Her aim was off, though, hitting the sidewalk nowhere near the offending neighbor.

"*Scheiss!*" she said, extracting Eddie's peashooter from beneath his bed, but Mrs. Thiele departed before Martha could load. Darting back downstairs, she saw Louisa, still a sobbing lump, on the living room floor.

"C'mon, Louisa! Stop crying and I'll let you beat me at checkers," said Martha.

"You let me beat you? Why you rat!" said Louisa.

"Ja, ja!" interrupted Martha, jabbing Louisa, who tickled Martha. "Herman, Eddie, Annie, make room for me and Louisa," said Martha. "I'm going to let Louisa beat me at checkers!" The incident was soon forgotten as they got lost in their games, which they were still playing when Bertha returned. Bertha stared at the children, rolled her eyes, and laughed.

Pfeiffer Household 1914: the year before the *Eastland* Disaster

At age 28, Emma, the oldest sibling, restricted her mousy brown hair in a tight bun, revealing her pockmarked forehead, and setting her pencil-thin lips in a constant frown. She had married a few years before, but still visited her parents' home regularly.

On a Friday afternoon, Emma and her mother peeled potatoes in the kitchen.

"*Mutti*, you have Martha too spoiled. She's a tomboy," said Emma to her mother. "Why do you let her wear Herman's trousers? I think there's something wrong with a young lady who dresses like a boy."

"She doesn't want to get her dress dirty while she works in the yard, Emma," said Bertha, waving at Martha, who was raking leaves.

Bertha walked out into the yard to speak with Martha just as Annie walked into the kitchen.

Emma looked at her mother and Martha working in the back-yard, harvesting what was left of the green beans, tomatoes, and peas. She turned to Annie and said, "Who will want to marry her?"

"Well, someone married you, so anything is possible," said Annie, who had been married for three years and was the mother of a small boy.

"You think everything is a joke, Annie," said Emma. "Martha is eighteen, and she acts like a child. She's a stubborn mule, much worse than Eddie or Herman. Why, she's as bad as a boy."

"Well, I think she's fine, and at least she doesn't bring a storm cloud with her whenever she comes into a room," said Annie. "Besides, you're married and miserable, I'm married and miserable, and, when Pa was alive, Ma was married and miserable."

"How dare you," said Emma. "Pa's only been dead a few months, and you talk about him this way!"

"I loved Pa," said Annie, "But you know as well as I do, he spent most of his time and money drinking. His drinking was more impor-tant than his family. And his temper. That time he broke Herman Junior's nose."

"He never did such a thing," said Emma.

"Oh, Emma, you were there. How can you say you didn't see that bash? Blood was everywhere! If Martha and I hadn't pulled him off Herman, it would have been worse. So, yes, I miss Pa, but I don't miss what he was doing to Ma, and to us," said Annie.

"Well, look at Martha. Look at you. You're wild too, and Martha looks up to you and wants to do what you do. You should be an example."

"An example of what? How to be a servant? How to be miserable? Oh, Emma, if you could stop being so jealous, you could see that Martha is different."

Emma shouted, "What? Me, jealous of her? And what do you mean, 'different'?"

"Martha has been drawing and writing her own stories since she was four years old. Look at all the little books she's made for the family. Look at all the plays she's written and performed. Why, she's just like Mary Pickford, and she sings like an angel," said Annie.

"So?" said Emma.

"She has abilities that most people don't have. Why, she could be anything," said Annie.

"Well, you take her to those places," said Emma.

"Museums and movie houses? Yes, I take her outside these four tiny walls, and why not? Her paintings are as good as some of those in the museums, and those sell for lots of money. And she's as pretty and as funny as any girl in vaudeville or the pictures," said Annie.

"Ach," said Emma, sweeping her hand, "You give her dreams and hopes. What can she do with dreams and hopes?"

Shaking her head, Annie walked into the next room where Martha and Eddie were playing with tops.

"What's wrong with hatchet face?" said Martha.

"Yeah," said Eddie. "Old hatchet face is in a bad mood again."

"She likes to complain," said Annie.

"About me?" said Martha.

"Yes," said Annie.

"Well, if I saw her face looking back at me in the mirror, I'd be in a bad mood, too," said Martha. Eddie and Annie chuckled.

ALTHOUGH MARTHA DUTIFULLY CLEANED, sewed, cooked, and baked, she yearned to run, climb trees, paint and draw, and go to saloons to see what men did in there. Waiting outside taverns with Eddie and Herman to intercept their father, and escort him home piqued her curiosity.

"Why can't I wear men's trousers?" Martha urged her mom. "They're much easier for running and climbing. I don't know why I wasn't born a boy! They have more fun, so maybe I'll be a boy. From now on, don't call me Martha—I shall be Mart!" God-fearing Bertha

Pfeiffer wanted to strike Martha to save her soul but ignored Martha's proclamation.

"You can wear the trousers, but only when you work in the back garden," said Bertha.

Bertha forgave Martha's infractions of propriety, blaming the child's rebellious ways on herself. "The sins of one generation passing down to the next," she thought.

Sycyna, Poland: Bertha's place of birth

Bertha's heart never lied, and for years—she dared not count them all—she had loved and longed for her sweetheart, Georg, who remained in the old country.

The last time they met, Bertha had just turned 21. Georg, at 22, liked to remind her he was older and wiser. Not much taller than she, Georg was forever brushing his long, sandy hair out of his blue eyes. They always met behind his father's barn and had been in love since they were children.

Georg, a farmer, was perpetually freckled, tanned, and had great, muscular forearms that he liked to lift Bertha with. She'd laugh and scream, "Let me down, or I'll kick you!"

"All right then, all right," said Georg, who gently lowered her to the ground as he lifted his hands to her braided blonde hair.

"It's soft, like corn silk," he said, stroking her hair.

Bertha breathed a deep sigh of serenity and leaned against Georg.

"Your eyes look like the bright blue skies today," she said, moving her face closer to his.

"Bertha!" her mother's voice pierced her heart.

Bertha jolted and looked up. There stood her mother, Maria, and her older sisters, Fredrika and Minnie, watching Georg and her. Bertha's insides melted.

"What are you doing?!" screamed her mother, but before Bertha could answer, her mother moved between her and Georg. Bertha, at 5'4" towered over her 4'10" mother and thought that would save her. She never saw her mother's hand coming toward her face until she tasted blood in her mouth.

"I will talk to your father," said Maria to Georg, who hung his head. Grabbing Bertha by the arm, Maria said, "You're coming home, and you won't see him any longer."

Maria Straszynska wasted no time cornering her husband, Franz, who was building a shed in the field.

Orphaned at two, Franz and his older brother were raised by Franciscan monks who taught him to bake bread, make wine, sew little finger gloves, and farm. A gentle, soft-spoken man with reddish-brown hair and dark blue eyes, Franz also had the air of a mystic, of someone not of this world.

"Georg is a good boy," he said after hearing Maria's tirade.

"Oh, Franz, stop being a dreamer. Georg has no money, and what can he give her but a hard life on a farm."

"Like our lives," said Franz. "Is that so bad?"

"I want her to have better, to live in the city," said Marie.

"Minnie and Fredrika have married farmers," said Franz.

"Yes, and look at how hard their lives are. Bertha is our youngest daughter. Don't you want something more for her?" said Marie.

"I want someone who loves her, and who is good to her," said Franz.

"I've been talking to August Pfeiffer about his son," said Marie.

"You think that marrying a blacksmith will be easier for Bertha?" said Franz.

"I've already made the arrangements," said Marie.

"You've made the arrangements," echoed Franz with resignation. "You will tell Bertha, won't you?"

With that, Franz continued building and praying.

The tall, slender, red-haired blacksmith's son and a blacksmith himself, Herman Pfeiffer had deep-set hazel eyes and a cleft chin.

Disobeying her mother was not an option, so Bertha and Herman married in Biedrusko, Poland in 1885. Bertha tolerated Herman, who was kind, unless he was drinking, but never forgave her mother for forcing this marriage.

"Herman is handsome, and he has some money. Don't you want

beautiful children?" proclaimed Marie, as if that was all Bertha needed. But Herman wasn't Georg.

Bertha had accepted her fate, but her shattered heart never healed, and the wound ripped open whenever she saw Georg working on his father's farm. They hadn't spoken since Bertha married but glimpsed one another when they were outdoors at the same time. She could live with the heartache, but a life with no joy and no hope was unbearable, and she began reading and re-reading the Bible, seeking comfort in the psalms, mostly. Then, she began having babies: Emma was born in 1886 and Annie was born in 1889. Bertha loved the children and busied herself with their care. She had been praying earnestly and sincerely since she was married for her heartache to end, and in early 1890, that prayer was answered.

Herman walked into the home with a letter.

"Bertha! A letter from my sister, Julia, and her husband, Robert," said Herman.

"In America?" said Bertha, who was making supper.

"Yes, in America! In America, everyone is rich, everyone has work. Robert is working in the mines in Johnstown, Pennsylvania. They said they need more workers and have secured a place for me. For all of us."

"Your sisters and their husbands and your mother, everyone can come! Bertha, why should we suffer here when it is so much easier in America? It is the land of opportunity, they say. We'll all go."

Bertha hoped America would make things better for the family, especially for her newly widowed mother. But something else impelled her—she needed to be far away from Georg. Someday, she feared, her heart would burst from the pain. Moving across the ocean meant that she'd never see him again.

"Have you talked to Minnie's husband about this? He was planning to move them all to someplace called Wisconsin."

"We talked. Wisconsin needs farmers, so I don't know what I would do there, but Johnstown is rebuilding after that big flood. They need people to work in the mills."

"I'd be afraid to live in a city that floods like that—and after what happened to your sister," said Bertha.

"But Julia was saved in the flood! That farmer pulled her out of the raging waters by her hair, with the baby still in her apron. Since then, they moved up in the hills where the waters can't reach if there's another flood. It's a large house, Robert says, and we can stay with them."

In November 1890, the clan emigrated to America. Herman, Bertha, and the children joined Herman's sister and her husband in Johnstown, Pennsylvania, while Bertha's mother and her siblings moved to Western Wisconsin. Five years later, Martha was born. Eventually, the Pfeiffers followed Robert and Julia again, to Chicago when Johnstown became inundated with steelworkers and iron-workers.

~

STARING AT MARTHA, Bertha muttered to herself, "So rebellious and headstrong she is. Like me."

Martha stormed off to the kitchen, whistling and yelling for the other children.

"Come on, everyone, I have something to show you!" shouted Martha.

Bertha knew her daughter would trick the younger children into doing her work by convincing them it was a great game. The rest of the household rode the coattails of Martha's buoyant energy. Although Martha was clearly a Pfeiffer, with her reddish-brown hair and fine features, she was not quite of them.

"I feel like she looks through me sometimes, as if she can see into me," Emma complained to her mother.

Bertha sighed, then smiled sadly, looking at Martha chatting nonstop to her siblings.

"Oh, let her alone, Emma," said Bertha. "The years will change her all too quickly and she will learn what life is about."

Annie and Martha

Martha shared neither Emma's harshness nor Louisa's theatrics. Like Annie, Martha loved living where many vestiges of the fabled World's Fair of 1893 were still intact. There were endless things to see and do in the White City. Whether riding streetcars, trains or the El to visit fairs, circuses and museums—Annie and Martha wanted to take it all in. Annie also struck up conversations with strangers and took their photographs with the Brownie camera that she bought in 1905 for two dollars.

Despite her family's protests, Annie, a Prussian Lutheran, married John Donovan, an Irish Catholic, in 1912. Marrying outside one's ethnic group, not to mention religion, was seldom done—but neither was leaving one's husband, which Annie would do a few years later.

Newly married with an infant, Annie grew bored and weary of her husband's verbal haranguing. She frequently asked her mother if she could have Martha help her.

"Just for the day, Mama," said Annie. "Oh, it's so hard to keep the house clean, and take care of the baby. Martha is so good with cleaning and making the baby smile."

Martha smiled at Annie, and Annie winked back.

"Ja, ja. You go with your sister and help," said Bertha.

"Come along, Martha, lots to do," said Annie loudly as she opened the front door. Martha could barely contain herself. Once Annie closed the door, Martha burst into laughter.

"Shah," said Annie, "Mama will hear you."

"No, she won't!" said Martha. "What did you do with Baby Wil?"

"He's with Mrs. Szbalski for the day, and she loves him. She lost her baby when we lost our Frieda, back in 1905 with the black diphtheria."

"Ah, Annie, now I feel like crying," said Martha.

"Wasn't Frieda the prettiest little thing, with her strawberry hair?" said Annie.

"Oh, I loved brushing her hair and making little curly Qs around her face. She would laugh and clap," said Martha. "She was so smart."

"I remember her blue eyes, they almost seemed too big for her little head," said Annie.

"The dress Mama made for Frieda's second birthday was so pretty. All lace and ribbons. It was beautiful!" said Annie

"I did some of the sewing!" said Martha.

"Then she got so sick. Little Frieda was buried in that lovely dress Mama labored over," said Annie.

"Mama cried for months and months. I didn't think she would ever stop crying," said Martha.

Annie said, "We all cried, and Pa just drank more."

Walking up to Annie's house, they both turned around.

"Let's go inside," said Annie.

"Yes," said Martha. "I have this feeling Mama is watching us."

"I have the same feeling. Let's leave through the back and catch the streetcar on Sacramento."

Once aboard the streetcar, the two women sat in the front.

"Annie, I want to sit by the aisle, or the wind will blow my hat off and muss my hair."

"What about me?" said Annie.

"You're already a muss," said Martha, nudging her sister with her elbow.

"That's what happens when you get married," said Annie.

"Just as long as you don't end up like Emma," said Martha, crossing her eyes and pulling down her mouth with her thumb and index finger.

"I would rather work at McCormick's factory before becoming that," said Annie.

"I thought you liked McCormick's," said Martha.

"Everyone called it 'the prison,'" said Annie. "Western Electric is much better."

"Ring the bell, Annie! We get off here," said Martha.

Annie stepped off, while Martha bounded off the trolley and began running.

"Come on Annie, let's hurry to the movie house," said Martha.

"I'll beat you there!" said Annie.

"Never!" said Martha, racing across the street to the movie house —a former butcher's shop. The counters and tables had been replaced by backless hard benches, ten in a row.

After buying their tickets, Martha said, "Quick, Annie! Let's sit up front."

"No!" said Annie. "The last time you did that, a boy threw an apple at you because you wouldn't take off your hat."

"If that boy is there, I'll thrash him, just like I did the last time," said Martha.

They scooted to the first bench and Martha smiled as she removed her hat. "I don't feel like chasing little boys today."

"What will we see?" said Annie.

"The sign said they are showing *The Adventures of Kathlyn*," said Martha.

"Oh! Kathlyn has such adventures, traveling all over the world," said Annie.

"We'll do that someday too!" said Martha.

Summer 1913

Annie and Martha shared a memorable summer when Annie took one of her many journeys away from her husband. Again, Annie told her mother she needed Martha to accompany her on the long train ride from Chicago to Falling Brook, Wisconsin, to stay on the farm with Aunt Minnie and Uncle Klaus. The ruse worked as it always had.

"It's only two weeks, Mama. Martha is so pale and could use some sun; besides, it will be good to get away from Chicago. It's so dirty. Why don't you come with us?" said Annie.

"And leave your father?" said Bertha.

"Why not?" said Annie.

"He would never let me, that's why not," said Bertha. "What about John?"

"Who?" said Annie.

"*Dein Mann!*" said Bertha.

"Mama, it's not good. He doesn't come home, and when he does," Annie paused, "I need to think. I need blue skies again and trees. I want Martha and me to milk the cows and feed the chickens with Cousin Amelia, just like we did when we were kids. Soon Martha will be gone and married."

"Who is she marrying?" said Bertha.

"Nobody. I'm just saying that we won't be able to do this once she is married," said Annie.

"If anyone will marry her!" said Bertha.

"Who wouldn't want to marry her? She's beautiful," said Annie.

"Ja, ja, but she still runs around like she's a boy," said Bertha. "She spends more time with you and her girlfriends than she does with any boy."

"Well, there's Henry," said Annie.

"Henry!" said Bertha. "Since he left for California, she has heard little from him. She ignores other men and tells me she doesn't want to be tied down. *Ja,* pack and tell Martha she can go."

Annie and Martha shared many childhood summers with Bertha's sisters and brothers on their western Wisconsin farms. Both loved the outdoors and farm life—something to which these two city girls were unaccustomed.

"I like the names of these places where Aunt Minnie, Aunt Fredrika, and Uncle Paul live," said Martha.

"The names?" said Annie.

"Falling Brook, Augusta, and Osseo, Wisconsin. They sound like cowboys and Indian names," said Martha.

"Remember those Indians that we met on Aunt Minnie's farm?" said Annie.

"Oh, yes," said Martha. "At first, they scared me—but just the way they dressed. I wasn't used to them, but they were so kind. They taught me, Cousin Amelia, and Aunt Minnie how to use berries to dye wool. Aunt Minnie made beautiful bedspreads from the wool and one of the Indians, a boy called Ben, gave me an arrowhead. I liked Ben a lot. Maybe I will see him again."

"I loved that we could wear boys' trousers, milk cows, ride horses, and collect eggs from the chickens and geese," said Annie.

"I wish I could wear trousers all the time," said Martha. "Oh, I just thought of something."

"What?" said Annie.

"Cousin Richard," said Martha.

"Oh," said Annie, knowingly.

"Do you think he's still mad at me for running off with his girl-friend?" said Martha.

"I don't know," said Annie. "You really shouldn't have done that."

"Nell and I were bored, and so we walked in the forest. There was nothing else to do after we finished working. We saw all kinds of animals and birds that we forgot to come back for a long time," said Martha.

"I know, but Richard thought you stole her from him," said Annie.

"Well, he was angry that she seemed to forget about him. He's very selfish, thinking that Nell should spend her time just with him," said Martha.

Falling Brook, Wisconsin

Annie and Martha were met by Aunt Minnie at the Falling Brook depot. Minnie, tall, slender, and tan, was Martha's favorite aunt. She and her husband, Klaus, had six children, all of whom were near the Pfeiffer children's ages. Some even shared the same first names.

Falling Brook, Wisconsin, population around 500 at the turn of the twentieth century, was a lumber and railroad village with a train connecting it to Chicago and Saint Paul. Yet, Falling Brook was a world away from Chicago. With one main road through town, the outskirts were still undeveloped woods and farm country. As much as Martha and Annie loved the city, they longed for open spaces and nature. There were no paved roads, and Annie and Martha laughed as they bounced up and down in the back of the oxcart toward the farm. Upon their arrival, they saw Cousin Richard staring at the cart.

"Hello, Richard," Martha waved.

"Cousin Martha, I have one thing to say to you—you stay away from my new girlfriend, or else!" said the gangly teenager.

"Or else what!" said Martha. "Or else I'll wrestle you to the ground like I did last time!"

"Oh! No girl is gonna wrestle me, particularly some city girl!" said Richard.

Like a tiger, Martha leaped from where she stood, knocking Richard to the ground. He was no match for the one-hundred-pound girl straddling his chest.

"Give up, or I'll wrestle you again," said Martha.

"Oh, I'm just letting you win," sneered Richard.

With that, he got up and started walking backward, giving Martha a piece of his mind. He didn't see Annie standing directly in his path with her foot extended.

Once again, Cousin Richard was sprawled out in the dirt.

The two weeks in Falling Brook passed speedily as the girls worked on the land, played in the haylofts, went to church, and had big Sunday meals.

Once back in Chicago, summer evaporated, giving way to a cold, gloomy autumn, where it rained daily. An influenza outbreak swept through Chicago, and on November 10th, just three days before Martha's birthday, Pa came home early. Bertha and the children had never known a time when he came home directly from work.

"*Was ist das los, Herman?*" said Bertha.

Herman complained of fever, sore throat, and headache.

"You must go to sleep, Herman," she said.

At eight o'clock she heard him coughing furiously from the bedroom and ran in to find him spitting up blood that covered his face, hands, undershirt, and their bedspread.

"Ach," she said, "*Kinder*, come in here!" Eddie, Herman Junior, and Martha came running into their parents' bedroom.

"What's wrong with Pa?" said Eddie.

"Why is Papa's face blue?" said Herman.

Martha came running in with a wet washcloth and began cleaning her father's face and hands.

"Herman," said Bertha to her son. "You must bring Dr. Kosinski now!"

"Yes, Mama," said Herman Junior, who ran to the house two doors down to summon Dr. Kosinski.

In just an hour, Pa babbled baby-talk, switching between Polish, Russian, German, and English. His temperature spiked, and he smashed a glass against the bedroom wall, screaming that the wallpaper flowers were turning into devils and would get him. Bertha, Martha, and Eddie tried restraining him, applying cold cloths to his face and body.

They heard the front door open.

Herman Junior and Dr. Kosinski entered the bedroom. Young Herman began crying while the doctor placed his black bag down and rolled up his sleeves. Judging by the cyanosis that had traveled from his ears and spread all over Herman Senior's face, the doctor knew.

"Why don't you go out to the kitchen and make yourselves tea," said the doctor.

"But doctor, I want to stay here," said Bertha.

"Please, Mrs. Pfeiffer. I need to try to help your husband," he said, opening his black bag. "Please close the door."

In the time it took them to warm the water for tea, Herman breathed his last rattled, jagged breath.

Herman was buried next to his infant daughter, Frieda, in Bethania Cemetery on Archer Avenue on another cold rainy day in February 1914.

"*Mein Gott,* what will we do?" Bertha cried.

"Mama," said Martha. "Please, Mama, don't cry anymore and don't worry. Yesterday, Uncle Paul and I walked across the street to Judge Stelk's house. Paul is courting his daughter, and the judge said that I could work for him as a housekeeper."

Bertha embraced Martha and cried.

"Don't worry Mama. Eddie, Herman, Annie, Emma, Louisa, and I will take care of you and baby Ida. I'll be here always," said Martha.

A YEAR PASSED since Herman Senior's death, and the Pfeiffer household continued with a few changes. Herman Junior married his sweetheart, Maggie, and moved down the road. Louisa married Bill and moved across town. Annie was still barely married to John, and Uncle Paul married Mary Stelk.

Martha continued working as a housekeeper for Judge Stelk and his wife. While housework bored Martha, the salary helped her family, and the humdrum routine gave her time to daydream. She wondered how much money she had to save before she could travel around the world.

In her less-inspired moments, she also talked of marrying Henry Sheck, the boy she walked home with after Sunday School at Saint Mark's Lutheran Church and played marbles and cards with.

Henry grew into an ambitious young man and left Chicago for California, just a year before, seeking his fortune. He told Martha he would return for her as soon as he became wealthy. Then, just a week ago, she learned her fiancé had married a California girl.

"Doesn't matter," said Annie, "You'll find someone new."

"Annie, I don't care if I do. I have more fun with my girlfriends—especially Heide—than with Henry, and he always got so jealous," said Martha. "I want to do other things."

"Like what?"

"Like travel all over the world."

"Too bad you're not a man," said Annie.

"It's not fair that I should not have dreams, just because I'm a woman," said Martha.

"I have something for you. A present," said Annie.

"You have a present for me?" said Martha. "What?"

"Well, I know how much you and Heide have been trying to get tickets for the Western Electric picnic, and I want to give you mine."

"The Western Electric picnic! Annie! How can you give away your tickets to the greatest social event of the century?"

Annie laughed. "Well, John doesn't like ships—I think he spent too much time on the ship from Ireland. Besides, that's next month in July when it's hot and I am not feeling well. Carrying this baby is harder than it was carrying Wil."

"Oh, you have at least a few more months to go, and you might feel better. Annie, are you sure? I would love to go, but you like to have fun too."

"This may be the first time in my life that I pass up an adventure," said Annie and the two sisters hugged.

"I've always dreamed of going across Lake Michigan on one of those ships."

"So, maybe this is one dream of yours that will come true!"

"Yes," said Martha. "Thanks to you. I have to run and tell Heide."

With that, Martha scurried out of the house, dropping the flyer for the Western Electric annual picnic, promising a band, dancing, food, and adventure on the Indiana Dunes—the eventual destination after the two-hour boat ride.

Friday Evening, July 23, 1915

"Mama, the dress is beautiful," said Martha, touching the white frock that Bertha hemmed.

"Quit moving, Martha," said Bertha, who stood up behind Martha as they gazed into the mirror.

"Mama, I love it. You are the best dressmaker, and not even Heide will have a dress this beautiful."

Annie came into the bedroom and said, "I have the loveliest sister!"

"Thank you again, Annie!"

"Just remember to do what I would do and enjoy yourself."

"I will," said Martha.

Saturday Morning, July 24, 1915

Kissing her mother goodbye, Martha left the house and met Heide by the streetcar on Saturday at 5:00 a.m.

By 9:00 later that same morning, Mrs. Thiele knocked on their door.

"Did you hear? Did you hear?" asked Mrs. Thiele.

"Hear what?" said Bertha.

"One of the ships turned over in the river! Everyone aboard was killed!"

"No! No! How do you know this? Someone is having a joke with you!"

"Bertha, it's no joke! Josephine Schmidt heard it from Celia down the street!"

"How does Celia know?"

"She heard it from the newsboys on the street."

Annie, Herman, and Bertha hurried out the front door to see their neighbors clogging the streets, chattering in multiple languages about what had happened. Everyone had someone who had gone to the Western Electric Company picnic.

Annie ran into the crowd, querying everyone she knew, and kept getting different stories: one boat fell over, all the boats fell over, one boat caught on fire. She found her mother talking with another neighbor and took her hand.

"Come on, Mama, come on in the house. None of them know anything."

Herman talked to some men to find out what had happened and returned home.

"It was one ship that capsized, and people were already aboard," said Herman. Bertha looked at him expectantly. "No one knows what happened, Mama. I'm sure that Martha is fine."

"I go and wait for Martha by the streetcar. She got on the streetcar, and she will get off on the streetcar. I will go and wait for her," said Bertha.

"But Mama," said Herman.

"Let her go," said Annie. After Bertha closed the door, Annie stared at Herman. "What did they really tell you?"

Herman hung his head. "There were thousands of people down by the docks, and as soon as everyone boarded the first ship, it kept swaying until it turned over on its side."

"Right in the river?" said Annie. "It can't be."

"Sal Bertoli said that people were thrown into the river. Rescuers are drilling holes in the ship to pull people out."

"What else did he say, Herman?"

"That the river is filled with dead bodies," said Herman, sobbing.

"What can we do now, Annie?" said Eddie.

"I have to go down there," said Annie.

"Wait for Mama to come back first. I don't think she could stand it if you were gone when she came back," said Herman.

The Pfeiffer Household, July 24, 1915

The family sat in the living room, boring holes in the walnut floor-boards with their eyes, wondering what they would do if Martha were dead.

The front door opened, and they all looked up expectantly. Instead, Bertha walked inside and stood, her eyes empty.

"I waited and waited for her by the streetcar. The streetcar comes, and she doesn't get off!" Bertha began wailing and praying in German.

Eddie bolted from his chair and punched his little sister, Ida, in the back of the head, and began pummeling her. Herman Junior separated Eddie and Ida. Scooping up Ida, Emma held her close, while Louisa ran to the back hallway, crying and screaming.

Amid the pandemonium, Annie stood and stared out of the window. Without them asking, she knew she was designated to carry out the deed. No one slept that night. Instead, they kept vigil.

Sunday morning, Annie moved her shoulder and winced in pain. She hadn't remembered falling asleep in the living room chair, but she must have. Others were still asleep, and Annie silently moved around the children on the floor, and her mother on the couch, grateful that the older woman was resting. Quietly putting on her hat, she carefully opened and closed the front door.

The sun glared. *How dare it shine today?* she wondered. Walking to the corner of 23rd Street and Sacramento, she saw the newsboys waving the *Chicago Herald* morning edition. Martha's photo shared the front page with many others, with the inscription, "missing," written underneath.

No, no, she was not missing. Annie would find her. *Martha will like this being on the front page of the newspaper. It will make her laugh.*

Walking to the streetcar stop, Annie observed dozens already there, waiting to make the unholy journey. There must have been extra streetcars operating that day, for one arrived just as she queued up. As Annie wandered to the back, a man stood, offering her his seat. She moved to the outside, fixated on the beautiful morning sky, swallowing hard.

A neighbor, Mrs. Z, as they called her, sat alongside her.

"Oh, Annie," cried the woman. "My Rudy and his wife and children were all on the boat."

Annie took the woman's hands in hers. "Our Martha," she explained and could say no more.

"The man over there said we have to go to the armory," said Mrs. Z.

"The Second Regiment Armory," the man sitting in front of Annie said.

"Why the Armory?" asked Annie.

"There's so many of 'em, so many people, they had to have a place big enough," said the man.

"So that is where we're going?" asked Mrs. Z.

"Yes," said the man.

The streetcar jolted and shuddered like a snappish horse rebelling against its destination. Annie worried that this jerking and bouncing would cause her to lose the baby she was carrying.

∾

MARTHA, just two nights before, was giddy! Chatting nonstop about the big Western Electric picnic, Martha complained about her shoes and argued with Heide, about which hat to wear.

Later that evening, Martha was so wound up that she spilled food, and dropped forks and knives in the kitchen. When she leaned over, Herman undid her apron. She laughed as she picked up her apron and punched her brother lightly in the stomach. "*Schlopphunas*," he called to her. She stuck out her tongue and laughed.

What would her mother do now, Annie wondered, with her husband dead not even a year and a half—and now, presumably, her nearly 20-year-old daughter killed on that ship.

Annie wanted to ask God why He cared so little for them. She sometimes felt out of place in her family, but she and Martha shared an intimate camaraderie. Annie's marriage took on increasingly depressing hues now that Martha would not be there to distract, no longer there for Annie to live through.

The women, more so than the men of this family, were the most perplexing creatures, even to themselves. From Bertha, who quoted scripture and incessantly read the prayer book, to cold, harsh Emma, to hysterical Louisa—they were all so different. Even little Ida already seemed destined for some of these eccentricities, what with her proclivities for play-acting. Then, there was Martha.

The streetcar slammed to a standstill, they filed out, and Annie stared at the endless queue of people. Blocks of people waited to enter the Second Regiment Armory, which looked like a medieval castle with its murky bricks and slivered windows. Eddie used to say they tortured people in there, and now she was sure he was right.

Annie stood in a line and saw neighbors, friends, and people from church. She nodded to a few, but no one spoke, and the only sounds came from wailing women. *Banshees*, thought Annie, remembering her Irish-born husband talking of the spirits that foretold death.

The rest waited until it was their turn to go in and identify their loved ones.

"I gave her those tickets—if I hadn't given her those tickets," Annie muttered. "Well, it's really Pa. Pa's to blame for following his sister and her husband to this godforsaken Chicago. We should have stayed in Johnstown, or have gone to Wisconsin with Aunt Minnie, Fredrika, and Grandma. None of this would have happened. Then baby Frieda would be alive, Papa would be alive and Martha."

The Makeshift Morgue - Second Regiment Armory

Annie was lost in thought when she saw it was finally her turn to enter. She wanted to run, to flee, but she couldn't. She mustn't. Once through the dismal castle doors, she saw the unbelievable and turned her head. The smell, the awful stench of death emanating from bodies lying on the floor, seared her nostrils and lungs. Annie grew dizzy, and her legs felt hollow.

Removing a handkerchief from her pocket, she covered her mouth, trying to breathe the fragrance from the talcum powder on her hands. Surveying the rows and rows of dead bodies, Annie was the stranger—one of the few living ones. Outstretched on the floor, were people she recognized: co-workers, neighbors, people from church, and friends. She started retching, and a Red Cross worker ran to her, asking, "Can you do this?"

Annie nodded, stood, and took a deep breath. Scanning the floor, she did not see Martha and half-expected to find her waving in the back, screaming, "Look, Annie, I'm here!"

Then she spied another Red Cross worker leaning over one of the newly dead, combing the corpse's hair, and sobbing. Annie knew. Walking over, she stood above the body and shook her head. The woman looked up at Annie, who said, "She is my sister."

Staring at her sister's body, Annie leaned over to stroke her hair. How did her red hair end up in shambles, and why was her beautiful white dress—the dress that Ma made for her with the intricate lace patterns—hanging in shreds from her body with only her corselets and shoes intact? The blanket barely covered her, and Annie put her hand over Martha's closed eyelids and touched her cheek, no longer warm.

Annie felt as if she was floating away, soaring through the ceiling to the clouds above, where she would meet Martha. Annie remembered Martha's embrace the day she gave her the tickets to the picnic. She had held Annie close and whispered, "Thanks." She remembered Martha's warm breath in her ear.

A man on the other side of the room was laughing and she glared in his direction. Then she saw the tears streaming down his face as his voice transformed into a howl. Annie looked at the Red Cross worker. "There are papers to sign," said the woman.

The Burial

Martha was buried on a warm afternoon in Bethania Cemetery, next to her father and her baby sister, Frieda. A death should be significant, but there were no neighbors, and no extra grievers except for the family. Martha was just one among the 844 who perished. There were not enough black sashes and coffins for the deceased, not enough undertakers, and assuredly not enough mourners.

After the burial, Annie opened the top drawer to Martha's chest of drawers. Martha's smell, the flowery aroma, overpowered her. For that moment, Martha was there, and Annie closed her eyes and inhaled deeply. "Martha," she said. Then Annie noticed an envelope in the drawer, partially obscured by handkerchiefs.

Lifting the unsealed flap, Annie removed a small locket that she gave Martha for her eighteenth birthday. She always wore the locket, but not on that day, and Annie opened it, staring at the tiny portrait of Martha that Annie had also placed there.

"My favorite sister," she said to Martha when she gave her this gift.

There was something else in the envelope--a photo that Annie had never seen of Martha and seven of her girlfriends, all dressed in men's clothes. Martha standing in the center of the adoring crowd, dangling a cigarette. On the back, she had written, "Say H.--Can you find me on here? Some kind of picture, I must say. Love, Mart."

Annie sat on Martha's bed, trying to understand. Martha told Annie everything, but not this. Why was she dressed like a man, and who was "H"? Annie took the photo and locket with her, for she didn't want anyone else, notably her mother, to find this.

FOR TWO MONTHS Bertha would wake up at 3:00 a.m., walk to the streetcar stop and wait for Martha. As far as Annie was concerned, this craziness had gone on too long, but when she tried stopping her, Bertha shrieked, "She left on the trolley, she will come back on the trolley." Sometimes Bertha would wait all day while the children cared for the house. After Bertha ceased going to the streetcar stop, she cried at night. During the day, she sat motionless in the living room.

Annie's daughter, Pearl, was born on February 4, 1916, and Bertha came to life again. Annie returned to her mother's home so Bertha could tend the baby, and Annie could leave her husband inch by inch.

In early 1919, Annie divorced her husband and continued working at Western Electric in Cicero. Seldom was divorce initiated by a woman then, but Bertha said nothing to Annie, and welcomed her as if she'd never been gone.

"It's my daughter," said Annie to her friend Edith. "Pearl reminds her of Martha and has made Mama come back to life again. I worried she would die along with Martha."

"It's been so awful," said Edith, who knew Annie from their Johnstown childhood, and now worked alongside her at Western Electric.

"My brother was on the deck when the ship turned over and swam to safety, but he is different now. Jumpy. In a foul mood all the time. I almost went on that ship, but I got there too late. I think we would all like to forget. My Frank is talking about moving back to Johnstown."

"Johnstown," said Annie. "Well, right now, I wish we'd never left it. Big city—Chicago! Lots of work for everyone! Hah! And we pay for it with my father's and two sisters' lives. I tell you this, Edie, in the night, after I put the children to sleep, I sit in the dark and dream of leaving Chicago."

"Annie, do you remember Fritz Otto from Johnstown?" said Edie.

"Fritz? You mean, Motorcycle Mike? Crazy Fritz?" said Annie. "I remember him. He would always get drunk and hop on that damn motorcycle. Half the time he'd crash and forget where he'd left it."

Edith said, "Once he had to use old Albert's cows to pull the motorcycle out of the mud. Well, yes, he was wild when he was younger, but you should see him now. He and his brother have a restaurant and two taverns. They are well off. And Fritz never married."

"Never?" said Annie.

"You know, Annie, he was asking about you when we last visited Frank's parents. Why don't you bring Pearl and Wil and take the train with us?"

"I'm not sure about that," said Annie.

"Well, at least write to him," said Edith.

So, at Edith's insistence, Annie corresponded with Fritz. A fellow ethnic German from Poland, Fritz invited Annie to visit when she accompanied Edie and Frank on the train to Johnstown in 1922. Fritz, at 32, was a year younger than Annie. He was nearly six feet tall with unruly dark blond hair, but Annie could never decide if he was handsome. His sharp, sculpted features gave him a distinguished look. Fritz, his brother Eduard, Ed's wife, and their two children lived in a 22-room-mansion on Grove Avenue in Johnstown, a former steel baron's residence.

Fritz and his brother did their time working in the coal mines when they first emigrated to Johnstown. However, both saw significant opportunities keeping the miners and other townspeople fed and watered and opened their first tavern on the outskirts of downtown. After that success, they opened another tavern and a restaurant.

As much as Annie wanted to leave Chicago, she could not abandon her mother. Since Fritz was not interested in taking on her young children, they agreed to wait until Annie's mother was better and the children were older. This began a seven-year, long-distance courtship.

Annie visited Fritz yearly where he would propose, and she would ask him to wait. They got to know each other primarily through letters. The marriage proposals and rejections were part of their relationship's ritual—so much so that in 1929, when Annie finally accepted, Fritz didn't believe it. This time she would leave Chicago—and her two teenaged children—to return to Johnstown, Pennsylvania, to marry a second time.

"Mama! You're getting married?" said Annie's 19-year-old son, Wilbert. At five-eight with dark auburn hair, a slight mustache, and prominent nose, Wil had grown into a nice-looking man.

"Yes, I'm getting married, and going to Johnstown to start over. I raised both you and Pearl by myself, and now that you're older, it's time for me to be married again."

"But Ma," said Wil, holding Annie's hand. "T'aint so, is it?"

"I've decided, Wil. And, you too, will have to decide."

"About what?"

"I know you want to farm with Uncle Klaus and *Tante* Minnie in Wisconsin."

"Yes, Ma. I don't want to stay in the city. I don't want to work for Western Electric or anyone. I'd rather live off the land."

"It's hard work," said Annie.

"I've been spending summers in Wisconsin since we were kids, Ma, and I know what it's like."

"Then, I won't keep you from your life. And don't keep me from mine."

"Johnstown's so far away," said Wil.

"You can come to visit, but I've made my mind up. Wil, you are a young man now and you have things to do," said Annie.

"And what about Pearl?" said Wil, pointing to the small girl standing in the corner. At thirteen, Pearl was already blossoming into a beauty. She inherited the beautiful eyes of the Pfeiffers, and the thick brown hair from her Irish father.

"Come here, Pearl," said Annie, and Pearl walked toward her

mother with her head down. She wrapped her arms around her mother and gently sobbed.

"Why can't I go with you?" whispered Pearl.

"You can come, only not now. Later. There's school and you need to stay to take care of Grandma," said Annie.

"Why can't I leave with you?" said Pearl. "Eddie, Ida, and Herman live here, and they can take care of Grandma. And Emma and Louisa only live a short distance away."

"Grandma needs you! You're Grandma's reason for living," said Annie. "I will come back, but I have to get used to it first. You finish school, take care of Grandma, and I will be back someday for you."

Pearl obeyed but didn't believe her mother. Not that her mother would deliberately lie, but Pearl possessed finely tuned perceptions and premonitions about people and events. She later explained that these prescient abilities were a natural outcome of being admonished to be quiet. She listened with her entire being and often retreated upstairs to her attic bedroom. Pulling the notepaper from her pillow, she spent hours writing.

The actual story was that Annie's fiancé, the nearly forty-year-old Fritz, didn't want Annie's children. This being his first marriage, he wanted it to be just the two of them: Fritz and Annie. At least, for the time being.

In 1929, Annie and Fritz Otto married in Johnstown. Annie worked with Fritz, operating his new grocery store, while he worked with his brother, running the tavern and restaurant. She loved being in Johnstown, getting reacquainted with childhood friends, and being away from anything reminding her of Chicago.

Wil moved to Wisconsin to learn everything he could about farming. He later married and relocated to southern Illinois. Pearl would take the train from Chicago to Johnstown during the summers to visit her mother and Fritz but was always told she could not stay.

Then, in 1931, at forty years of age, Annie gave birth to a baby girl, Helena Anna.

Looking into her baby's face, Annie felt worthy of a second chance at life and spent hours telling the infant the stories of her life in Chicago. Stories of her parents, her brothers and sisters during the happy times. And she could safely recount the story of Martha to the baby until it didn't hurt her heart so much. The baby cooed and gurgled while listening to her mother's voice.

"I promise you," said Annie to her baby. "I promise to tell you these stories again when you are old enough to understand, and we'll go back to Chicago and see everyone again."

Fritz was in the dining room and the baby asleep nearby. While she was making tea, Annie felt a throbbing pain in her heart take over the left side of her body.

Hearing the crashing pot, Fritz raced into the kitchen to find Annie on the floor.

Pearl got the news and deliberately took a later train, fearing that her mother would ask her to remain and raise her baby sister. She couldn't do that. By the time Pearl reached Johnstown, Annie was dead. She was buried June 27, 1934, in Grandview Cemetery near the graves of the unknown dead of the Johnstown Flood. Pearl returned to Chicago the day after and regretted taking that later train for the rest of her life.

Pearl continued living in her grandmother's house and listening to stories of her family's past. While adults talked, she pretended to ignore them, but Pearl would cook or clean while remaining in earshot of a conversation.

Mrs. Thiele pointed to Pearl and said, "Dumb?"

"What do you mean?" said Bertha.

"She just works, says nothing," said Mrs. Thiele.

"She's not dumb," said Bertha. "Pearl is just polite and shy. She doesn't interrupt."

And the older women grew very close and, instead of arguing, they now swapped stories about days gone by, preferring the past to 1930s Chicago. Pearl overheard their stories about her grandfather, baby Frieda, Aunt Martha, and her mother, and would write them down in her journal after everyone had gone to sleep.

Pearl was nineteen—Martha's age—when Bertha died. She

subsequently moved in with her Aunt Ida and Ida's husband, a Chicago police officer, who lived a few streets down.

Yet there was no time to nurse grief since the world beckoned. Pearl had grown into an elegant young woman with lots of friends, including Henrietta Pospisil, who worked as a clerk for the *Chicago Herald*.

"Why don't you write for the *Herald*?" said Hettie.

"You won lots of writing awards in school," Hettie continued. "We have some gal reporters, and besides, you know you would get too bored just typing."

Pearl wrote a few filler pieces, and readers noted how penetrating and poetic her features were. Her ability to coax stories from everyone she interviewed won her more work. Her articles for the daily were gaining attention, but her fledgling writing career ended in 1939 after she married Mike Pospisil, Hettie's brother.

Now Pearl again confined her writing to her bedroom.

Johnstown 1934-1950

Meanwhile, in Johnstown, Fritz was raising his daughter, Helena, with help from his brother's family. Helena met her older half-siblings, Wil and Pearl, a few times when they scraped together enough to take the train from Chicago to Johnstown. Other than Christmas cards, she had no contact with her aunts and uncles in Chicago.

When she was thirteen, Helena saw Chicago for the first time when she took the train to see Pearl. All she remembered from that trip were the "enormous buildings everywhere."

But that was just once.

Chicago, like Helena's mother, remained a distant tendril of a dream. Helena grew up, graduated from high school, then attended and graduated from the University of Pittsburgh in Johnstown, majoring in science. A couple of years before graduation, she met Joe Vrabel, a local radio personality—someone that Helena never heard of. Helena's cool reserve intrigued Joe, who was accustomed to throngs of fans. She iced up further when she discovered he was known as "Handsome Joe, the Singing Cowboy."

A classical music aficionado, Helena told Joe that she didn't care for "hillbilly" music.

"And Vrabel? What's that? Hungarian?"

"Slovak, sort of. My dad was actually Rusyn, and my mom is Slovak. My parents immigrated from Hungary or Austria, but I think it's Czechoslovakia now," said Joe.

"Whoever heard of a Slovak Singing Cowboy?" said Helena.

"You have!" laughed Joe.

As Joe attempted to court her, Helena learned they had a lot in common. Besides being children of immigrants, Joe, like Helena, was also minus a parent.

Joe's father died when Joe was thirteen, and he and his seven siblings quit school and worked odd jobs to support the family. Joe tried different trades and failed at most, except playing guitar. A brilliant musician, Joe formed a country band and hosted a daily radio show in Johnstown. Joe had never been west of the Mississippi, but that was beside the point. He loved the song "Riding Down to Santa Fe" and, so, *Handsome Joe and his Santa Fe Trailblazers* were born.

Joe's persistence melted Helena's reserve and they married after she graduated from college. As for Chicago, Helena didn't think about it. Nor did she think about her mother or Pearl during those years. No point to it. She was now married and had her own life.

Annie's death should have ended the story of the Pfeiffer family and the *Eastland* Disaster, except that Helena also had a baby girl.

2

ANNIE'S GRANDDAUGHTER

The children belong to her (the mother's) clan, not to the clan of the father. She is the spiritual teacher of the child, as well as its tender nurse, and she brings the developing soul before the Great Mystery as soon as she is aware of its coming.
—Anonymous

Saint Paul, November 1997

While drifting off to sleep, a familiar dream replayed:

She was no older than six, walking hand-in-hand with her dad toward a ship moored on the Lake Erie shore in downtown Cleveland. He moved her in front of him so they could ascend the narrow gangplank. Midway up the ramp, she froze, stopping everyone behind her. Terror swirled around her, cutting off her breath for a moment, but then she wailed louder and louder until her dad scooped her up and barked to the people behind them to "Get out!" and ran back down the gangplank.

"What's wrong? What's wrong?" he said.

"We'll die!" she screamed. "We'll die if we get on that boat!"

A THUNDERING KNOCK at her apartment door jolted her awake, and her body pulsated as if it were a heartbeat. The clock on the nightstand read 4:00 p.m. She'd seemed to have been dreaming for hours, but it was only minutes. Sleeping at night was pointless, so she tried catnapping after work. Also, pointless.

Leaping from bed, Zara took a running slide on the shimmering black bra on the bedroom floor.

"Holy shit, whose is this?" she said, dangling and dropping the lacy undergarment. It could belong to one of three women she was dating—none of whom knew the other existed. At least, that's what she'd hoped.

The knocking persisted.

"I'm coming!" she shouted.

Glancing in the bathroom mirror, she ran her fingers through her disheveled blonde hair. "Geesh, I look like Billy Idol after an all-night bender. Time for a haircut!"

Zara spotted the mail carrier through the peephole and opened the door.

"Whoa, Sandy, you scared the crap out of me," said Zara.

Sandy, the compact, fresh-faced, buzzed-cut mail carrier, always made a point of seeing if Zara was home during her deliveries.

"Well, you got this big envelope here from Chicago, and I didn't want to leave it on your doorstep," said Sandy, thrusting a crumpled 10 x 13 brown Kraft envelope into Zara's solar plexus.

"Uh, thanks," said Zara.

"You know, Dayton's is having a furniture sale," said Sandy, peering into her apartment. "I mean, your place screams Peace Corps volunteer!"

"Now, what more do I need besides a kitchen table, couch, TV, entertainment center, and bookshelves?"

"How about furniture that matches?" said Sandy.

I'm not a materialist. Besides, don't you have mail to deliver?" Zara enjoyed flirting, and thought if Sandy knew her age, she'd run screaming—or maybe get off on it. No one ever guessed Zara's age. Nearly 40, she was often mistaken for 30—and even younger— thanks to her martial arts training and early morning jogging. `Friends mentioned that she resembled Annie Lennox, but she thought she favored the *Home Alone* kid. She even dressed in cargo pants and oversized sweaters, giving the illusion of being much younger. Oh well. She enjoyed extended adolescence. Life owed her an extra decade, anyway.

Walking down the hall, Sandy paused, turned back, and said, "Hey, are you going to the Townhouse on Saturday night? It's Jill's birthday."

"Ha, since when do I miss a party?" said Zara.

Sandy grinned, "So, who you gonna take?"

"That could be a problem, so maybe I'll go solo."

"Save a dance for me. You're my favorite dancer, Zara."

"Yeah, yeah," said Zara.

"Hey," said Sandy. "I, uh, read the article—the one you wrote about your dad. It was really good. I cried. My dad died too, a couple of years ago."

"Thank you, Sandy," said Zara, closing the door.

THE YEAR BEFORE HIS DEATH, Zara sensed that her dad, Joe, would not be around much longer. She envisioned the memorial tribute she would write for him. "The Last of the Singing Cowboys" paid homage to his status as a local country and western radio star in Johnstown, PA in the 1940s. It was her personal, funny, heartbreaking story of being his daughter. *The Saint Anthony Park Bugle*, a monthly community newspaper, published the piece. She had been freelancing for *The Bugle* since the late 1980s, while finishing her master's degree at Martin Luther Seminary.

She never dreamed his story would touch so many. Out of respect and embarrassment, she omitted the multiple nervous breakdowns that plagued him during his last decade. Her dad felt a failure much of his life because, according to him, he never made it to "the big time" as a musician.

"Well, Dad," she thought. "You have your fifteen minutes now, even if it is in Saint Paul, Minnesota."

But dead is dead, and she'd never see him again—not in this life or any supposed next life. Although she missed the comfort of faith, Zara had outgrown organized religion and couldn't fortify herself with that delusion, even if she tried.

Still, she missed him so much, and life was out of order and askew without him. And what was going on with that dream she kept having about them boarding the ship? What the hell was that about?

Even sleep provided no refuge.

Sitting at her dented 1970s Formica kitchen table, Zara studied the envelope.

Who would send me something from Chicago?

Examining the wobbly handwriting and the return address, she shouted, "Oh my God! It's from Aunt Pearl! I thought she was dead!"

No one ever described Zara's maternal side of the family as close.

Slitting the bulky envelope with scissors, Zara peered at a manuscript wedged inside and shook it. The hefty document thudded on the table, but a yellowed newspaper clipping also began cascading toward the floor. Zara caught it midair. *So fragile— like butterfly wings.* The masthead read, *Chicago Herald*, Sunday, July 25, 1915, with the cutoff headline presumably reading *Eastland Tragedy.*

Eastland Tragedy? What is that?

She stared at the four photos, below the heading, of three young men and one gorgeous young woman, whose picture was circled in black pen. The inscription, "missing," was listed below her name: Martha Pfeiffer.

Pfeiffer? Annie Pfeiffer was Mom's mother, but who's Martha?

Whoever she was, the camera loved her, and Martha returned the favor by tipping her lampshade hat and flashing a side-glance smile. Her eyes were light, maybe blue, or green, wide, and slightly almond-shaped.

Placing the clipping on the table, Zara removed the handwritten note attached to the manuscript.

~

November 1997

4233 W. 88th Street

Hometown, IL

My dear Niece Zara,

Greetings from Chicago. You are probably surprised to hear from me. It's been a long time since we've communicated, but I felt you should have this family history that I wrote.

Your mom said you are a writer now too, and she sent me some of your articles. They're very good, and I'm proud of you!

And now I thought you might find it interesting to learn about your mother's mother and her side of the family. I don't think you know much about them, and it's time you knew their stories. It's too bad your grandmother died when your mom was only three. I was fourteen, and so I remembered a lot about her.

I will do my best to explain everything. It's all new information for you, and I want to make sure I don't confuse you.

After your grandmother died in 1934, I lived with her mother (my grandmother) and my aunts and uncles in Chicago. Your mom was a baby and stayed with her father, who was your grandmother's second husband, in Johnstown.

Well, honey, I'm getting up there myself—82 years next February. Before I go, I wanted to pass this history on to someone who will do something with it.

Oh, and the newspaper clipping—I felt you should see it. This is your grandmother's younger sister, who is your Great-Aunt Martha. She was almost twenty years old when she was killed in 1915 on that ship, the *Eastland*, in downtown Chicago. There were 844 people, including Martha, who lost their lives that day.

It was a mournful time for the family. Your grandmother had to go to the morgue to identify her body. Just about everyone in Chicago had lost someone on that day. But you'll read about that in the genealogy. Or is it a family history? I am not sure.

Aunt Martha died just before I was born, but her photos always make me think of you. Whenever I saw pictures of you, I said, "She's going to be just like Aunt Martha."

ZARA LEANED back in the chair and shook her head.

The closest she ever got to Annie Pfeiffer, her maternal grandmother, was at Grandview Cemetery in Johnstown, PA, when she accompanied her parents. She was about three or four.

"That's my mother," said Zara's mother, Helena, pointing to a tombstone. Zara's eyes widened while clutching and digging her nails into her mom's hand. How could she have a flesh-and-blood mother, and her mother have an enormous chunk of rock with writing?

Helena, a tall, willowy redhead, leaned over and stroked the tombstone while holding Zara's hand. Zara noticed tears forming in her mother's eyes. Helena wiped them away and stood up straight.

Zara felt Helena's grief and but didn't know how to soothe her. Instead, she scurried away and ran toward the rows of unmarked white gravestones that belonged to the 777 unknown dead killed during the 1889 Johnstown Flood.

Zara extended her arms and rushed up and down the rows. Grandview Cemetery was a splendid playground, and Zara loved scampering and studying the rolling hills that cascaded to the valley below.

Her dad shouted, "What are you doing, Zara?"

"Playing with my friends here, Daddy," said Zara.

Joe Vrabel, short, dark-haired, and olive-skinned, was the mirror opposite of his wife. A child of Rusyn and Slovak immigrants, Joe's family had ethnic pride before it was cool. Immigrant families of his generation mostly worked at "being American" by ditching residual accents, telltale clothing, and anything else that screamed "immigrant." Helena was incredibly self-conscious about being the child of ethnic German immigrants from Prussia. Not Joe!

"It's in the blood, it's in the blood," proclaimed Joe. "Look at my family—musicians, artists, actors, and fortune-tellers. Your Mom's family? I don't even know what they are. Pollacks? Germans? She won't talk much about 'em, but I'm easy on her. I mean, she never had a Mama. My Pap died too, but at least I had my Mama. Your Ma's family, they're not happy. Spend too much time putting on airs, trying to be what they're not."

Joe, a musician, fronted a country-western band and hosted a daily radio show in Johnstown, where he dedicated songs to Zara.

Although Zara's parents moved to Cleveland when Zara was about three, they made the six-hour drive to Johnstown most weekends.

Zara loved the Johnstown weekends, but detested the "big spooky house," where her mom grew up.

~

AFTER HELENA'S MOTHER DIED, she and her father, Fritz, moved into a mansion owned by his brother, Eduard.

Fritz's brother's wife, Gertrude, was ordered to care for Helena. Aunt Gertrude performed her obligations with bitterness, treating Helena like a servant. When Helena wasn't cooking, she was endlessly cleaning, "Whether something needed cleaning or not," declared Helena.

Aunt Gertrude also pandered to her adult son, Emil, an inveterate drunk and gambler. Emil was married, divorced, and remarried at least twice and returned to his parents' home after losing most of his money. Several times, he neglected to wed the mothers of his various offspring and could count on his mother to cover up for him.

Years later, Helena recounted: "Emil was okay until he started drinking and all bets were off. Once, he brought a bobcat into the house. He was too hammered to realize the animal shredded his arms and face. Uncle Ed shooed it out, but not before it destroyed Aunt Gert's handmade curtains."

While her mother unpacked their luggage in the guest room, Zara left. When Helena realized Zara was missing, she ran out the front door and found Zara sitting on the steps.

"Zara!! Never leave without telling me where you're going," said Helena.

"I want to stay at Grandma's with Daddy," said Zara.

"We'll visit your grandma later. You don't want to stay there! If you do, you'll have to go to the toilet outside," said Helena.

"I don't care! I want Daddy and Grandma," said Zara. "Grandma's kitchen always smells good, and Uncle Rip and Ted are funny. Grandma really loves me, too, and the way she talks makes me laugh."

Helena shook her head and asked, "Grandma talks with an accent because she was born in Czechoslovakia, so don't laugh at her speech. But just a minute! Why don't you want to stay here?"

"This house is too big and scary. And everyone seems mad," said Zara. "Then there's her in the living room. How come no one talks to her?"

Helena grabbed Zara, pulling her up to the large wraparound porch. "Zara, I told you—that's Cousin Emil's wife."

"Well, what is wrong with her? Why does she stink, and why is she so sad? Why does she sit in that chair with wheels by herself all day? How come none of the rest of them talk to her? I don't like them," said Zara.

"I told you, Zara," said Helena through clenched teeth. "Cousin Emil got drunk and hit her over the head with a whiskey bottle. He paralyzed her. She can't walk."

"I'm not going back in there. They're very bad people. Have Daddy come and take me to Grandma's house."

Zara emerged victoriously and, from that point on, Zara stayed with her dad at her grandma's whenever they visited Johnstown.

～

SHE BANISHED UNCLE EDUARD, Aunt Gertrude, and the others to the outer recesses of her memory years ago, and now they returned. Her sweeping exclusion of her mom's family was because of these wretched people.

No wonder Jane Eyre was Mom's favorite novel.

Because of that crew, she never expected that the other branch of her maternal line would be worth pursuing.

Something else stood out as she reread Pearl's note.

Wait a minute. This Eastland Disaster killed how many? Eight hundred plus in downtown Chicago?! That's insane! How can that be?

Did Pearl get it wrong? Nonsense! Once a journalist, always a journalist. She would have confirmed this. But how could something of this magnitude occur in Chicago without me hearing of it?

EVEN WHEN SHE was in grade school, Zara longed to visit Chicago, which seemed a thousand times more fascinating than Cleveland.

The Second City contained the proverbial stuff of legend: The Great Fire, the Iroquois Theatre fire, and the Saint Valentine's Day Massacre, to name a few. Why was the *Eastland* Disaster excluded from that litany of catastrophes?

How could the City of Broad Shoulders fail to hold the 844 lost lives?

Zara combed the family history, which Pearl typed in an uneven Courier font that pressed into the paper.

Gad, someone still uses typewriters?!

The first page listed thirteen rows of names, birthdates, birthplaces, death dates and places of death.

She wondered who these people were until she saw her grandmother's name.

Wait a minute! These are my great-grandparents and their children. Holy hell! My grandmother had a HUGE family!

While studying the document, she felt overpowered by every emotion in her being. Her maternal family history blew like Vesuvius, and the ashes of the past engulfed her.

Zara saw even more names in the chronicle—all strangers. Yet, they belonged to her, and she to them. The words soon seemed to mutate into an unfamiliar language—she'd been gazing far too long and forgot to blink.

Let's look at this: my great-grandparents, Bertha Straszynski and Herman Pfeiffer, were born in what is now Poland. Both died in Chicago. How in the blazes do you pronounce that name? Stras-in-skee? Hmm. Even Pearl spells it a couple different ways in the document. Safe to say my great-grandmother was Polish. Mom insisted her family was German, and I can't wait to drop this bomb on her!

Her grandmother's parents and siblings were born in different places, and her Great-Aunt Martha, like her, was born in Johnstown. The only difference was Martha's family left Johnstown for Chicago while Zara's left for Cleveland.

We were born in the same city, albeit decades apart.

She turned a page and read that her great-grandmother's siblings, and her great-great-grandmother, initially moved to a small village in western Wisconsin called Falling Brook.

Back up! Western Wisconsin? Just across the border? She'd remembered Falling Brook as one of those blink-and-you-miss-it towns from her travels to and through nearby Eau Claire.

Oh, my Lord! I'm only a stone's throw away from an ancestral land. I moved to the upper Midwest to escape family and start with a clean slate. What did I do?? Does this happen to other people? I'm afraid to turn another page in this thing!

～

When I Was a Child, I Thought as a Child

Zara's mom's family was a jumbled mess, and from a child's viewpoint, they made no sense.

Why was Mom's mother dead? Why was Aunt Pearl only a half-sister to her mother? What is half of a sister, anyway? And why did Pearl live so far away?

Her mother shrugged. "Well, I've only seen my sister a few times in my life."

What? Weren't sisters supposed to live together, at least during some juncture in their lives?

Zara loved rummaging through her mom's shoebox of photos, and especially enjoyed looking at the pretty-as-a-picture Pearl. Zara's mother characterized her older sister as "resembling Norma Shearer," referring to the 1930s actress.

Zara was six when she first met Aunt Pearl, who took the train from Chicago to visit Zara's family in Cleveland. She eagerly anticipated the arrival of a movie star! They waited at the train station in Cleveland's Terminal Tower, which had seen better days. Its floor was faded green, the walls an even more faded brown, and the wooden benches yellowed and worn. The air reeked of mildew, cigarette smoke, and old newsprint.

The stout, grey-haired woman who stepped off the train bore no resemblance to her 1930s photographs, and Zara wondered what happened to her.

Pearl was wonderfully cordial, and Zara overcame her disappointment by forcing a spirited rendition of the song, "Chicago." Aunt Pearl enthusiastically applauded in response.

Zara later asked why Pearl didn't resemble her old pictures, and Helena tried to explain what the passage of time did to a body.

Zara could not comprehend this.

Thus, her mom's family remained an enigma—from the stone grandmother in Grandview Cemetery to the half-a-sister in faraway Chicago. On the other side, there was that repulsive bunch living in the haunted house in Johnstown. Something was off about her mother's family, and it terrified Zara. She wanted nothing to do with them.

The memory pileup continued.

~

Zara's Parents' Home: 1960s

Zara was eight, watching the *Wizard of Oz* with her parents and sister. Her grandfather, Fritz, who had just moved in with them, was asleep in his rocking chair, next to the fireplace.

"Now, remember," said her mother. "This movie is just make-believe, so don't get scared of the witch or anything else."

"I won't," said Zara. "But *she* will because she's such a baby!"

With that, Zara's little sister, BeeBee, lunged toward her. Although smaller than Zara at that point, the curly haired BeeBee tackled Zara and knocked her on the floor.

"That's it," said her dad. "One of *yintz* sits here with me on the couch. The other sits with Mom in the chair."

Amid "Somewhere Over the Rainbow" Zara noticed a young woman in their dining area—her upswept thick brownish-red hair embellished with a huge green bow several times the size of the woman's head.

She thought it was her mom's cousin, Dodi, since she often dropped in unannounced, except this woman was too young to be Dodi.

Why did everyone ignore the woman? Didn't they see her?

As Zara stepped toward the visitor, an icy shiver shot down her spine and back up to the top of her skull.

The woman's attire—a white blouse with a high frilly collar and a long skirt, down to the ground—was all wrong! A grandma might wear this, but not a young woman. The woman then smiled, and Zara's terror transformed into fascination as she peered into the woman's enormous, welcoming, sea-green eyes.

Zara had never seen such a pretty woman before and was over-powered by shyness and felt butterflies tickling her stomach. The woman moved her lips, but Zara heard nothing.

Zara's mom finally glanced up from the TV.

"What are you looking at, Zara?"

"The pretty lady in the old fashion dress," said Zara.

She waited for an explanation, and her heart sunk when her mom said nothing.

Tousling the child's hair, her mom laughed, "You have a lively imagination, don't you?"

The young woman vanished, and Zara thought her mom was right—except Zara always knew what was real.

Helena Vrabel taught biology and chemistry at a private school in Cleveland and suffered fools not at all. If she couldn't see it, it simply wasn't.

Still, Zara knew what she saw. Even if it made no sense, that woman was standing in her parents' dining room—and then she disappeared. She'd thought about it sometimes, but eventually chalked it up to "one of those things."

Oh, it can't be. The woman in the newspaper clipping was the same one she had seen years before. Zara knew it. She battled with herself, though, since any proclivity toward mysticism or the supernatural was shamed out of her decades before.

"You don't want anyone to think you're like Magda, do you?" Helena frequently warned her daughter.

Enter Aunt Magda

Magda Vrabel Velgyak, her dad's sister, was Zara's favorite aunt. Zara's mother, however, was no fan.

"Tell your sister to stop filling Zara's head with superstitions and ghost stories! No wonder she can't sleep," said Helena.

"Ah, Helena, lay off! It's Magda's way, and besides, we grew up on those stories. We believe them!" said Joe.

"Well, I don't like it one bit," said Helena.

IN THE MID-1960S, the newly widowed Magda, by then on the cusp between middle-age and old-age, sported a bleached blonde Veronica Lake-style hairdo and tooled around town in a lemon-yellow 1965 Mustang convertible—leaving a path of speeding tickets in her wake.

Her hair, protruding eyes, and dramatic gestures caused a striking resemblance to Bette Davis in *All About Eve*, enough so that even strangers frequently approached her for autographs. Magda obliged, and years later, Zara wondered how many "Bette Davis" autographs on eBay actually belonged to Magda.

Magda, though, was a star in her own right—a still-life artist and renowned psychic. Kids in the family loved being around an adult who didn't act like one. Magda was fun, mischievous, irreverent, and told spellbinding tales.

Although Helena forbade Magda's yarn spinning around the children, Zara seized every opportunity, when the two were alone, to wheedle tales of the supernatural from her. It fitted that Magda lived in a hundred-year-old, two-story home next to Kotecki Monuments on Cleveland's southeast side. At Kotecki's, workers cut and engraved marble and granite tombstones at all hours. Magda's house was also two blocks from Calvary Cemetery, a sprawling memorial park established in the 1890s for Cleveland's Roman Catholic population.

As a child, Zara often spent weekends with Magda. Once, they stayed awake most of the night, drinking cocoa while the rain walloped the tin roof, nearly drowning out the clanging hammers next door at Kotecki's. That night inspired Magda to tell more stories.

"On the night my sister died—well, I didn't even know she was that sick," said Magda. "I was sitting in the kitchen, in this very chair, when a flash of yellow light blasted through this door, and then shot out the kitchen window. It looked like a glowing baseball, except it didn't shatter the window. Then, not five minutes later, I got the call that Eva had died."

"This window?" Zara stood up and walked to the window. Magda's backyard was overflowing with a crazy quilt of flowers—primarily peonies, marigolds, and wild roses. She welcomed weeds, which grew alongside basil, thyme, lavender, bee balm, fennel, and garlic, which she used for potions and salves.

"There must be something about this window," said Magda, standing up alongside Zara. "Another time, I was standing here, putting dishes away and looked out. I saw this little boy, probably about six or seven, playing in my backyard."

"How'd he get in? You keep everything locked up," said Zara.

"Exactly," said Magda. "So, I opened the door and said, 'Hey nudnik, what are you doing in my yard?' and it was then that I noticed it."

"Noticed what?" said Zara.

"His clothes. He wore the style of cap and short pants little boys wore in the 1920s. Kids don't dress that way now. Even though I've seen many strange things in my life, I still get rattled. When I looked at him, he smiled but was so pale—almost transparent. Then—*poof* —he disappeared into thin air!"

"Really and truly?" said Zara, craning her neck to get a closer look at the backyard. "Have you seen him since? Do you think he was a ghost?"

"Of course he was a ghost," said Magda. "Later, I went next door to talk to Sol and Fanny. They'd lived here since 1915, so I figured they would have known something. They remembered a family with lots of kids living in my house. When the Great Depression hit, the father couldn't find work and became violent, beating the wife and the kids. Finally, his temper got the best of him, and he beat his six-year-old son to death."

"A dad beat his little boy to death? Was that the little boy you saw?" said Zara.

"Sol and Fanny described him as a pale, sweet-faced blond boy named Hank who was killed around 1930," said Magda.

"You haven't seen Hank since?" said Zara.

"As soon as I knew the story, I told Hank that I saw him and knew he was dead. I told him to go home and said, 'Hank, your mother and brothers and sisters are waiting for you.' I told him that his father was sorry and would never hurt him again. Haven't seen Hank since."

"Gee," said Zara.

"The dead who walk among us mean no harm. Sometimes they're lost and need help from those who can hear or see them. Maybe *help* is the wrong word. They need assistance to make their last journey home," said Magda.

"Have you helped—well—assisted lots of ghosts?" said Zara.

"I've been doing it most of my life," said Magda, sighing. "Then there are the others."

"Others?" said Zara.

"Yes, there are those who...hmm. Oh, dear. This is hard, Zara. I'm not used to talking about my work. I just do it," said Magda.

"Tell me."

"Remember when you told me how frustrating it is when your parents and sometimes friends don't always understand you."

"Yeah, I hate that," said Zara. "I really hate that!"

"Makes you feel isolated, right?"

"Yes."

Well, that's what it's like for the others who are spirits of a different stripe. They come because they want someone to listen and understand them, and they want to accomplish something, too."

"Accomplish something," said Zara. "You mean like a job or a homework assignment?"

"Yes, that is a good way to describe it. These spirits aren't lost, but they have left some things undone, and need support from people like me. When we help them, we help ourselves. Well, Zara, this is a lot for one night. Let's go to bed."

Zara nodded solemnly but didn't understand. Zara slept upstairs in the attic bedroom, and the persistent rain lulled her to sleep while she thought of Hank, the ghost boy, and other spirits who needed Magda.

By morning, the rain stopped, and the aroma of coffee, eggs, and bacon filled the house. While eating breakfast, Zara asked Magda if she read Tarot cards since Zara had just learned about them from a *Zolar* magazine.

"Cards!!" Magda harrumphed. "Cards??! Cards are for amateurs!! I don't read cards. I read *you!*"

Zara shrunk back as Magda moved into her face.

"So, tell me, Zara, what do you think?" asked Magda.

"About?"

"Life—here and hereafter," said Magda.

"I dunno," Zara sighed. "I'm almost twelve, and I thought I'd know everything by now, y'know. Sometimes I feel kinda grown up—well, almost. Then sometimes, everything scares me," said Zara.

"What about death?" said Magda.

"I'm definitely scared of that, too. My mom said when you die, you turn back into chemicals, but still."

Magda shook her head, "Come on, child, let's finish breakfast and then take a walk."

While walking, Magda was quiet, letting Zara prattle on.

"I think about God, Aunt Magda, and, you know what? I think I'd like to be a minister someday so I can help people too. But don't tell Mom, okay?" said Zara.

"A minister?! Of course, dear. I forget you were raised in your mom's religion and aren't Catholic. Then, that would be a good thing for you, provided you have passion and love for it."

"But my mom," Zara's voice sank. "She thinks people who believe in God are foolish."

"Well, what about your dad?"

"You know Dad! He'll go along with Mom."

"Ah, never mind," said Magda. "If you want something badly enough, darling, you won't need anyone to buy into anything. You will just do it. That's how life works. Oh! We're here already."

Zara was too busy rambling to notice where Magda led them.

"What are we doing here?" said Zara.

They faced the imposing wrought-iron gates that opened into Calvary Cemetery.

"We'll walk around, darling! There is no more peaceful place than a cemetery—the city of the dead!! And look at how the trees grow

here. You will never see more majestic trees than the ones in a cemetery. There's nothing to be afraid of here."

Zara surveyed the marble headstones and walked up to one.

"They made this one at Kotecki's," said Zara.

"Yes," said Magda.

"Aren't you afraid of ghosts and stuff, Aunt Magda?"

"Remember. I'm of the Carpathian Mountain people—the dead
and the living—we see them all. There's no difference. You're part of
these people, so you can see them, too."

Zara shuddered. "If it's all the same, I'd rather not. Are they here
in the cemetery, Aunt Magda?"

Magda looked around and shook her head. "Not today. They
rarely hang around cemeteries."

"You've never been afraid of the dead?"

"Listen," said Magda, "people think of me as wise. To this day, they
still come from everywhere for psychic readings, and to contact the
dead. When I lived in Johnstown, I had to move twice to get away
from them, and they still found me!! Well, I suppose they're right—I
am wise. That said, I will tell you that one sure thing, you'll always
have more to fear from the living than from the dead. I prefer the
dead."

Not knowing how to respond to Magda's proclamation, Zara
changed the subject.

"I wish I could talk to my mom the way I can talk to you."

"Sometimes, it takes years for mothers and daughters to develop a
common language. This was so with my daughters," said Magda.

"My mom is just so serious," said Zara.

"She's sad, darling. She covers it well, but she's very sad."

Zara stopped walking and said, "Sad? Why is my mom sad?"

"Oh, let's see what I can see about your mother."

Magda leaned against a large oak and closed her eyes. Zara never
disturbed Magda when she did this—this was her "private consulta-
tion time" when she talked with the spirits.

Opening her eyes and nodding, Magda said, "Well! Of course! My
guides tell me it's easy to figure out. Your mother's family is so tragic."

Zara thought of her mother as reserved and intense, not tragic!

"Well, her own mother died when your mom was just a baby—no older than three, I believe. Then, Fritz, your grandfather, was ill-equipped to be a mother and a father! So, he moved in with his brother and the brother's wife, Gertrude. Gertrude took care of your mom, but I can hardly say she raised her. Awful woman. Good Lord, I used to call her the Bride of Frankenstein. Cruel, cruel."

"Yeah, she had bad vibrations! But why did my grandmother die so young?"

"She had a heart attack, or so they say. I tell you what, though—a heart doesn't attack anyone, much less itself. More correctly, her heart shattered."

"Shattered?"

"Didn't your mother tell you the story?"

"I don't know much about Mom's family."

"There's more to your mother's family than her father's relatives —those people you didn't like. Your mom had a mother whose people were quite high-spirited. You may be more like them than you realize."

"Really?"

"Ask your mom about the story," said Magda. "Well, on second thought, maybe don't. She might get angry with me for mentioning it. We'll just keep it between us."

"All right," said Zara.

"Here's the story. Your grandmother's younger sister, who was about 20 years old, was killed. I don't know the details, but she was on a ship that capsized or wrecked in Chicago. And your grandmother blamed herself."

"What?!"

"Yes," said Magda, closing her eyes again. "I can see it as it's happening. Your grandmother blamed herself for her sister's death."

"Aunt Magda, I'm confused. Who died in a shipwreck in Chicago?"

"Your grandmother's sister. She would be your great-aunt and...." Magda closed her eyes again. "Not yet? Not yet, you say? I understand.

My guides tell me I can't talk about it with you. The timing isn't right."

"But I want to know about what happened," said Zara.

"The story is too heavy for you to carry now. But when the time is right, they promise me that the story will reveal itself. In fact, I can tell you she'll be waiting for you. Yes, your great-aunt just told me she will wait for you," said Magda.

"Who's waiting for me? And what's this about a shipwreck in Chicago? I want to know about it now."

"No!! This family story would be lost on you. Forget about Chicago, shipwrecks, and your great-aunt. Spend your time growing up and enjoying being young. You have so many places to see, people to meet, and adventures ahead of you! Your biggest challenge will be to know yourself. And after you've grown into who you're supposed to be, your great-aunt and her story will be there for you."

"Tell me more, please. I'm so confused," said Zara.

But that was the end of that conversation. *Fini.* Zara never pushed Magda. But after Zara went home, she asked Helena about the story.

"Magda exaggerates!" said Helena.

That was as much as Zara gleaned from her mother. For a long time, Zara wondered if Magda concocted the story.

WHEN SHE WAS 15, Zara's home life changed. What was going on? She didn't know. Her formerly convivial father receded into the background, seldom speaking. He instead spent hours watching TV or repairing things around the house.

Her mother also transformed from a supportive champion to a competitor who seemed threatened by her oldest child's "otherness."

Helena mocked Zara's interests. When Zara joined the Lutheran Church youth group, Helena reminded her of a cousin who gave so much money to the church that she eventually had to live in her car. "Be careful, or you'll turn into a fanatic like Cousin Leona," said Helena.

Shame and hurt gave way into white-hot anger, and Zara said, "Well, you're the one who strong-armed me into getting confirmed at that church. So, it's your fault!"

That terminated this line of insults, but there were always more.

When Zara told her mom that she joined the church choir, Helena said, "Don't you have to be able to sing?"

Talk about a sucker punch! Zara knew she could sing, since she was making money performing solos at church weddings. Her parents never knew.

Then there was BeeBee, who, at age ten, began hanging out with older kids, most of whom were Junior High and High School dropouts. They weren't of the 60s *Zeitgeist* but simply greasers who grew their hair and had an excuse to drink. As the sixties kept swinging, BeeBee joined in. Instead of attending school, BeeBee spent time at concerts and hanging out with various low-lifes. When she was arraigned for truancy, the family was "sentenced" to counseling. There Zara learned that her dad's father didn't die in a mining accident—he killed himself.

She grabbed BeeBee in the hall and said, "Did you know Grandpa killed himself?"

"No!" said BeeBee, "How could I know? But that was a long time ago, and it doesn't affect us."

"I'm not so sure," said Zara

~

ZARA PRACTICALLY LIVED at church and shared little with her family. By then, they weren't much of a family anyway, all living separate lives, only sharing the house.

The church was a lifeline for Zara, where she forged deep friendships with other kids and their families. She taught Sunday School, led the youth group, and performed folk songs during communion. The pastor became a surrogate father, who she visited often and confided in.

She shared a special bond with her first boyfriend's parents and siblings. She liked him enough but was in love with his entire family. They were the family she wanted to have, not the ones she'd been stuck with. She even resembled them enough where she was often mistaken for one of their children.

Zara began plotting her future escape, with Aunt Magda as her co-conspirator.

Thank goodness for Magda.

Zara called Magda, then walked to the corner to catch the Broadway bus that dropped her off about a half-mile from the house. Zara walked up the front steps and heard Magda shout, "I'm in the kitchen!"

After hearing Zara's litany of complaints, she said, "Stop! It's your turn to listen to me."

"Okay," said Zara.

"This is important. Promise that you won't stay here. I mean it! When you are old enough, get out of Cleveland! It is not your home, and you have other places where you're supposed to be."

"Where?"

"That's for you to figure out, Zara. It's different for young women now, and you have more opportunities than I ever did. If I were young now—well—just take advantage of that freedom and manage it well!" said Magda.

Zara's eyes widened.

Magda continued, "This is dicey. Very dicey but must be said. My guides have told me you can never be yourself here. It would not be —well, umm—healthy."

"Your guides said that?" said Zara.

"Let me explain. Your mother loves you, even though you don't see it now. But she doesn't understand where she ends, and other people begin. If she'd only had her mother, instead of that crew who raised her. We don't blame her, Zara, but we also can't let her suffocate you with her fears. She needs to deal with those. As you grow more independent, she may dig her hooks in deeper, and you'll need to stand up for yourself. She can't be with you, and she can't be away from you. Oh dear, why is this so hard," said Magda.

"What's hard, Aunt Magda?" said Zara.

"Oh, darling, you're a strange little creature, aren't you? Much older than your years, but you're in that hinterland: no longer a child, but far from being an adult. Still, you feel the nudging from your own guides now, yes?"

"Wait a minute, Magda. I have spirit guides? How did that...?"

"It's hard for mothers. We, too, have lessons to learn. There's a poem by Kahlil Gibran that says, 'Your children are not your children... they come through you but not from you, and they belong not to you.'[1] We mothers need this frequent reminder. But back to you— you will indeed meet the ones who have been guiding you since you were born."

"Meet?! I have spirit guides like you do?" said Zara.

"Of course. Most are ancestors who act as silent partners. They help us, but most don't believe that they exist. But for you, it's different. You, like so many women in our family, seem to recognize them. You hear their voices," said Magda.

"Magda, I have never heard voices!" said Zara.

"Not literally, maybe. But you respond to them anyway."

"I'm lost."

"You were born on a bridge—not a literal bridge—but you stand in between worlds. One foot in the light and the other in the mud! Oh, don't worry. I'm the same, and that's why I recognize it. You pick up on people's essence, don't you?"

"I guess."

"You know who's good, who's bad, and who's harmless. You can see around corners sometimes, and you often know what will happen next. I'm right aren't I?" said Magda.

"That's right," said Zara. "I thought everyone had that."

"Maybe they do, but some of us have finely tuned abilities. This runs in families, and you've inherited many centuries' worth of abilities. Did you know we had an ancestor who was burned at the stake for being a witch?"

"What? A witch? Like in Salem?!"

"No, no. Our people didn't immigrate until the late 1800s, so we missed Salem. I'm sure we would have burned had we been there, though. Accusing women of witchcraft is a long-standing church tradition that dates back to Europe to at least the 14th century. Maybe earlier. Long ago, in what is now Czechoslovakia, our ancestor, a woman called Maxinka, was burned as a witch in the 1500s."

"No kidding??! Oh my gosh. Was she really a witch?"

"Don't know. But at the very least, Maxinka was an herbalist and healer, according to family lore. She was born in my mother's village of Štítnik," said Magda.

"Magda, are you a witch?"

"What do you think?"

"Well, I think you are, but you're not evil or wicked."

"Oh, goodness, Zara. I hope that stereotype of the wicked witch dies off at some point. You come from a long line of women who would be considered witches."

"But the churches say witches are going to hell."

"And most churches are run by men who purloined the magic long ago, and then condemned and killed women practitioners for using the very devices they stole from them. Oh, let's change the topic. I could go on forever about this."

"So, am I a witch then?"

"Well, it's a family tradition, but take a hint from me and don't talk about it with people, especially your church friends. They won't understand or approve, and you might be put in danger. Learn to grow that garden of knowledge inside of you. Trust that when you need the right person to help you—living or dead—they'll arrive."

"What am I supposed to do?"

"Right now, keep getting good grades and find a nice out-of-state college to attend. You'll need to leave to find yourself, and don't ask me to explain that contradiction. Life is full of them. Once you're away, you'll find your strength. Oh, it won't be easy—it's not supposed to be. But you will learn what you need to move to the next step. And after you graduate college, keep moving. You'll find another place that will feel like home," said Magda.

"Magda, explain. Please! I truly don't get what you're talking about. And you're kinda scaring me," said Zara.

"When you arrived in this incarnation of life, you didn't come in alone," said Magda. "You also brought other selves—ancestors who act as your guides. They, in turn, also have their own capabilities honed from various lifetimes."

"You've lost me there, Magda. I'm just me! There are no other people involved."

"How do you think your father could pick up a guitar and play it with the skill of a virtuoso? He never had lessons, and he still can't read music," said Magda.

Zara answered, "He was born with a talent, and he always said...."

"... It's in the blood!" Magda completed the sentence. "And where does that blood come from, darling?"

Zara stood in front of Magda, smiled, and shook her head.

"You're co-sharing your life with many ancestors. Not sure why you have so many, but they're all very creative. I don't know the ones from your mother's side, but you have our musicians and our—umm —wise women. Each brings talents—tools—for you to use and nurture, and when you use them, the ancestors get a chance to shine. You're never alone, but it won't be easy since these creative selves will try to claim center stage during various periods of your life."

"Well, I'm already playing the guitar, but what about my other talents?"

"They arrive when the timing is right."

Zara sighed.

"But, when they show up, get a handle on them, or they might tear you to shreds!"

"What?!?"

"Oh, don't worry! If you couldn't deal with them, they'd never have accompanied you through this lifetime," said Magda. "You will grow into a very capable and, yes, a sagacious woman."

～

PEARL'S MANUSCRIPT turned her world on its axis. Between newfound family and long-forgotten memories, Zara couldn't concentrate.

I wish Magda were here, but maybe she is.

Magda knew that I would have died had I remained in Cleveland. I needed a safe place far away to reinvent myself, and Minnesota seemed brilliant. The scattergun bullying and shaming by family, church, and society ground me into a pulp. Just the word "family" incensed me. Yeah. "Family" is the first place they look when there's a murder. Even if they didn't value me, I valued myself and filled that void with a fantastic family of choice.

But what about now? Of all the places I could have moved, I was lured to the land of my maternal ancestors. Why them? Could that explain why so much of the upper Midwest felt so welcoming? Hmm. Magda was onto something—we're watched over by someone. Lots of someones maybe. But who or what was doing the guiding? I always thought it was God, but maybe it's someone a lot closer.

ZARA STOOD up from the table and stretched. Pouring another cup of coffee, she looked out her kitchen window, oblivious to the snow piling up on the trees. Instead, she relished the long-ago times with Magda, although those memories also involved reliving her pain-filled teenage years.

Yech. How did I survive?

No matter how she tried, she couldn't extract the ship disaster story from Magda. Still, she got something much better: a promise that the disparate portions of her life would eventually converge. And apparently, this was the "someday" that Magda had foreseen.

Her family, and even close friends, sometimes labeled her a dilettante, since she was always exploring new things. "Why can't you stay the same?" said one of her friends. "You're always changing!"

Maybe it was because of all of these people that I carry inside my blood.

Was it possible that her ancestors' lives spilled over into hers? Maybe she needed to look closer at the Human Genome Project that hit the news a few years ago. She never thought of the ancestors needing expression—she assumed people were born with certain talents, and there was nothing more to it.

Zara had been an actor, singer, and writer, with the writer being the constant. She'd worked as a freelance journalist for over twenty years for newspapers and magazines while juggling a full-time job in software development. She graduated with honors, with a BA in business, mostly to prove that she could do it. Otherwise, she had little interest in that field. And her MA in systematic theology gave her a chance to study something she liked, but the only fallout was that she lost the faith she once had.

Zara flipped through Pearl's family history, returning to the pages about the western Wisconsin relatives.

This is still unbelievable.

She again studied the names of her great-great-grandmother and great-great-aunts, and uncles.

Why did they immigrate to western Wisconsin and Minnesota? And why did I follow them here?

She couldn't count the number of times she'd passed through, or stayed in Eau Claire, Wisconsin, which was adjacent to the towns listed in Pearl's document. Why did she keep going back there? She loved day trips, or even weekend getaways, in or near this university town, where the rolling hills and confluence of the Eau Claire and Chippewa Rivers created a lovely ambiance. It was literally where the buffalo once roamed and where the Ojibwe lived. And now she knew it was also where her ancestors' blood and bones fed the earth.

She opened her notebook and wrote. *I have now entered my personal Twilight Zone.*

3

SOMETHING'S COMING, SOMETHING GOOD

Z ara recalled a fateful—or maybe fate-filled—trip she'd taken
in '81 with Karol, her then-girlfriend, when they drove from
Ohio to Minnesota.

~

*THE WEEKLONG VACATION was to be a romantic getaway, but once we
reached Chicago, the atmosphere shifted from light and airy to slightly foreboding. I'd never visited Chicago, but it was so familiar. Everything felt
surreal as we walked around the city. The ringing in my ears grew so loud
that I thought I might pass out. I paused at every building—captivated by
the surroundings. This annoyed Karol, who said, "It's just a city. Haven't
you ever seen a city before?"*

*High voltage energy waves surged and flooded my senses. The jolts
subsided, becoming a piercing, relentless pain as the hours passed.*

*I tried explaining it to Karol, who laughed. "We have to get you out
more often! You're such a bumpkin."*

*I often felt alone in that relationship, but finally saw how cruel this
beautiful woman was. What did I see in her? I asked if we could leave a day
earlier than planned.*

"Why not," said Karol laughing. "Once you're in the Wisconsin back-woods, you'll probably feel at home."

Many a word spoken in jest.

Driving west on I-94/I-90 out of the city, I glimpsed downtown Chicago in the passenger mirror with the words, "Objects in the Mirror Appear Farther Away than They Actually Are" imprinted over it. "No shit," I thought.

~

EVERYONE SHOULD DRIVE *through Wisconsin once just to see an endless stretch of prairie paradise with its majestic stretch of forests, rock forma-tions, rolling bluffs, curving roads, and small towns.*

The tranquility lasted about four hours.

It happened again right around Eau Claire, Wisconsin, about 70 miles east of the Minnesota border. Again, that deja vu feeling flooded me, but this time, I corked my emotions. I couldn't take any more putdowns.

Senses and emotions crashed and crescendoed until we were just outside of St. Paul.

"That's it! Stop the car. Here! Here!" I said to Karol, and she pulled into the parking lot of Our Lady of Angels Church, near the 3M facility.

I leapt out of the car, lifted my arms, and exclaimed, "I'm moving here. It's right and I belong here."

"How can you be so sure? You haven't even seen the Twin Cities!" said Karol.

By then, the relationship was past resuscitation, and I cared little for her judgments.

"Doesn't matter. You don't have to see a place to know it—this is home! I've been praying for direction and knew something was on the way. My intuition has been firing on all cylinders during this entire trip. I couldn't figure out why until now."

I needed a place that was just mine and no one else's. This was surely it. Home was truly where my heart was.

Zara never doubted that she made the right move—it was intoxi-cating, starting afresh where she knew no one. It was also the place where she could reassemble the splintered fragments of her existence.

4

ONE-WAY TICKET

Oh damn! It's 8:00 p.m., and I forgot to prep for tomorrow's 5:00 a.m. with Ford! Damn it!!

Racing to her bedroom, she logged onto her computer and, while it booted, she returned to the kitchen for one last look at the document.

The countless relatives in Chicago, Wisconsin, and Minnesota cast a new light on that 1981 trip. Could that explain her burning compulsion to move to the upper Midwest?

I research everything within an inch of its life! Knowledge and information are power and if I have enough of both, I'd survive, and do well in the world. All I need are facts. But this is the first time information is not translating into knowledge. What's going on here?

And she began crying.

What if everything I've done was wrong? Oh Dad, you weren't much for giving advice when you were alive, but I could sure use some now. I don't know what's going on, or what to do.

~

WHILE IN GRAD SCHOOL, Zara worked for an adoption agency, writing biographies for those seeking information about birth parents or birth children. She lost track of how often the birth children's lives paralleled those of their birth parents—even though they had never met. She always thought families were inconsequential in determining the paths one takes in life. Those narratives—and now the evidence in a document on her kitchen table—showed her otherwise.

That missing 1/4 piece of my ancestral pie apparently mattered.

Desultory recollections synchronized like the patchwork quilt that her grandmother made for her mother. There was no point in stopping or censoring them.

Forty-something is not a good time to wonder who you are! I thought I solved that years ago.

Deciding to forgo sleep, Zara brewed some coffee and continued examining Pearl's manuscript.

Pearl wrote:

"Martha Elizabeth Pfeiffer drowned on the *Eastland* on 24 July 1915, where about 844 people lost their lives. Western Electric had a yearly boat excursion picnic. Martha didn't work at Western Electric, but her sister, Annie, did and gave her the tickets. Martha and her girlfriend planned to attend the picnic. The boat was still moored in the Chicago River when it overturned. Western Electric never again had a company picnic."

AN EXCHANGE OF PAPER—PAPER!—CHANGED everything. That's what Magda meant. My grandmother gave her sister the tickets that Martha paid for with her life. If that exchange hadn't happened, had my grandmother gone on the Eastland instead, maybe none of us—my mom, my sister, her sons, and I—would be here.

Oh, Martha. Is that all that's left of your nearly twenty years on earth? A newspaper clipping and a few paragraphs? Why didn't I ask about my grandmother's family before this? Why did no one, besides Magda, hint at Aunt Martha and how she died?

Damn! I wish Elly were here. She could help sort this out.

Zara's best friend, Elly D'Angelo, was working in New York City all week. She couldn't wait for her return and had to take action. Despite trepidation, she called Aunt Pearl.

The phone rang at least ten times and Zara was ready to hang up when a lilting voice answered the phone, "Praise the Lord!"

She sounded like a young girl, and Zara paused before saying anything.

"Um, Aunt Pearl, is that you? It's Zara calling from St. Paul."

"Oh, honey," said Pearl. "You must have gotten my family history document."

"Aunt Pearl, I'm sorry that I haven't contacted you before. I'm blown away by your writing, and that newspaper clipping. I mean, I did not know about my grandmother and all those relatives in Wisconsin. And Aunt Martha. Thank you for the story about her."

"Well, honey, the Lord told me to start writing and to send that to you. Otherwise, all of those stories are going to get lost."

"I was shocked to hear from you. I mean, I thought you were...are you doing, okay?" Zara decided not to mention that she thought Pearl had died.

"Oh, just the usual aches and pains that come with old age. Nothing serious, but let's face it, at my age, you don't know when your time will come. You know it's sooner than later."

"It's great that you're doing well, Aunt Pearl, because I'd like to make up for lost time. There's so much I want to know about you and our family. Especially Martha."

"Let's see now. In 1914—the year before your Aunt Martha was killed—her father, Herman Pfeiffer, died. I think it was from flu, but I'm not sure. At the time of her death, Aunt Martha worked as a housekeeper for Judge John Stelk, who lived across the street from our house. You know, I lived in that same house with my grandmother until I got married!"

Pearl continued, "Martha had a fiancé named Henry Scheck, who moved to California for work. But after he got there, he married someone else. Your grandmother worked for Western Electric and was pregnant with me at the time of the yearly company picnic. It was supposed to be the event of the year, taking the boats across Lake Michigan to Michigan City in Indiana. Well, your grandmother gave the tickets to Martha and her girlfriend instead. The girlfriend died, too."

"You said 844 people were killed? If that many died, why on earth haven't I heard of this? I mean, the *Titanic* has had like five movies about it, and it's part of American folklore. Why not the *Eastland*? Why not something that happened in Chicago?"

"Well, that's a good question, Zara, and I don't know why. But the number of casualties was correct."

"Sorry. But I can't believe this was forgotten," said Zara.

"It's hard to believe such a thing happened, and then was erased from history."

"I didn't even know I had a Great-Aunt Martha, much less know that she died on a ship that I'd never heard of. Geez. No one ever told me."

"Don't blame your mom. She didn't know. I knew. But it took me this long to talk about it," said Pearl.

"There's so much that's been unleashed in the last few hours since I've been reading this!"

"Well, sometimes God keeps things hidden for good reasons," said Pearl. "The time has to be right."

"My Dad's sister, Magda, used to say that all the time!"

"Martha's buried not too far from where I live. She's in Bethania Cemetery, along with her parents—your great-grandparents," said Pearl. "Maybe you'll come to visit me sometime and we can see it together."

"That would be great!"

"Since you're so interested, I'll send you whatever photos I have of Martha. I have the cutest picture of her and a bunch of her girlfriends dressed in men's clothes. She kind of reminds me of you here. Would you like to have that picture of her?"

"Men's clothes, did you say?" said Zara.

"Oh yeah, it's so sweet, too."

Zara's heart raced with hope. Could there be someone like her in the family, another gay person? She may never know, but born-again Aunt Pearl just supplied some supportive evidence.

After they hung up, Zara called her sister BeeBee in Ohio, excited to report the findings.

"That doesn't mean she's gay," said BeeBee.

Poor BeeBee. She lanced a wound that was decades in the making.

GROWING UP, Zara's family often ridiculed her tomboy appearance, putting it mildly. She was treated like a pariah, made to walk behind her parents when they were out, because she resembled a dirty little boy.

As she got older, other relatives—not just her immediate family—treated her like a child because she refused to marry and join "the fellowship of suffering," a club that most of her female relatives were life members of.

"You don't want to be a spinster, do you?" asked her Aunt Dodi.

Alone in her room, Zara railed, "God, I didn't make myself like this. I love the church and I've accepted Jesus, but this doesn't change who I am. You supposedly don't make mistakes, so what in the hell is this?" Zara despised those flashbacks.

"Y'KNOW, BeeBee, everywhere you look in the family there's someone like you, married and unhappy, but married—or remarried," screamed Zara. "And for this one damn time, this one goddamn fucking time, there's possibly someone in our family who might have been like me. Just one person. ONE! Someone I could look up to. Someone who might have been my friend and approved of me!! Is that asking too much?!"

"Whoa, Zara. God! Get a grip," said BeeBee.

"You'll never understand," said Zara, slamming the receiver down.

Zara seldom retaliated when subjected to family derision, but this time was different.

She wanted acknowledgment from family, who always treated her as if she were less than them. No matter what her accomplishments—putting herself through undergrad and grad school, graduating with honors, being a published writer, a musician, and founding a theater company—that didn't matter. To them, she was less than a woman, a grown-up, even a human! All because she was different.

And they wondered why she had left.

I HAVE no gift for you, save this wounded memory.—Zara's Journal

Writing was Zara's best therapy, and she would again write all night.

Growing up, I was really different. I know many people feel like the outcast, the black sheep in the family, but I, however, actually was.

"A girl child should prefer dolls, not melt them on top of the furnace," I heard an aunt say.

"She likes guns. Then, get her guns," my father laughed.

My little sister just cried, wanting a playmate. "Why is she more like a brother than a sister?" she whined, "My other friends' sisters play tea sets and dress-up—not her though." She broke down, so forlorn, so disappointed in me. Everyone was disappointed in me.

I wanted to be accepted, but not as much as I wanted to be true to what my insides were telling me. "Family" was becoming synonymous with pain and heartache.

When relatives gathered, I roamed from room to room, seeking someone like me to validate, lead, answer, and give direction. I always worked best from models, but there were none. Even Magda would sometimes side with the rest of the women, betraying me further.

The talk of women was vapid and ridiculous. When they weren't discussing curtains, diaper pails, soap operas, and neighbors' morals, they turned on me, telling me how I could improve my looks and act more ladylike.

The female and male relatives settled like cream separating from the milk. No surprise that I always ended up with the men then, coonskin cap over my head and toy gun in my hand.

"Whatcha gonna be when ya grew up, child?" asked an uncle.

"A boy, I hope," I often said.

The men were a little rough sometimes, and I wasn't entirely at ease there. No matter where I was in a room, I always kept one eye on the women from afar, hoping for a human face, a sign that someone would welcome me. There was none. Instead, the great divide grew deeper.

I SPENT part of one summer with my uncle and his wife when I was seven or eight. His wife seemed offended at my gender-bending adventures, and one afternoon, Sally Lou grabbed me by the shoulder and hurled me into the kitchen chair.

"I know what you are!" she proclaimed.

I wish she would have told me.

"And I want you to know that you can't be that way."

What way? I wondered.

"Do you know what they do with women who dress in men's clothes? They put them in jail!"

My face burned. Shame is a lump of hot coal aimed for a heart to keep it from beating the truth back. I wasn't doing anything bad. I was just being on the outside as I felt like on the inside. All my life, I was told to be honest and tell the truth. Now, I was being told not just to tell a lie, but to BE a lie.

That was one of the defining moments of my life. Second only to my mom and Aunt Magda, I looked up to Aunt Sally Lou, desperately wanted her approval. No more.

I swallowed hard, didn't say a word, and decided not to need Sally Lou.

Deep inside, I knew I had a good heart, mostly because I'd read a Classics Comic Book about Joan of Arc. I thought we had a lot in common. They made her a saint, and she dressed in men's clothing and fought wars. I knew someday that I would fight evil too because my other hero was Superman. These were good ideals, so how could I be bad?

I wouldn't wait around for canonization. Instead, I would leave home as soon as I grew up. I was itching to escape, and my biggest dream was to go far away and recreate myself in my image. I did it several times. There was no point in staying around my family.

5

LIVING IN THE PAST

Your ancestors battle for you every waking moment. I mean that, literally.
—Arch Oboler

While driving to work, Zara felt more unsettled than usual. Initially attributing the malaise to early spring doldrums. She hoped she'd feel better when winter finally receded, but her depression wasn't weather-related.

Her work life was like an awful movie that needed a new scriptwriter. This morning, she cajoled and threatened herself just to get to the office.

How will you pay rent? How will you pay your bills?

"But you have a good job, an exciting job," her neighbor once said. But Zara's career, or rather the company she worked for, was in free-fall. Producing industrial videos and multimedia training sounded glamorous, except that Zara and her fellow producers had little control over projects and the budgets.

Then there was the company. Located in a high-rise near the Mall of America, Johnson and Smith Training had been in business for 10 years despite itself. Zara took the position over a year ago, ignoring industry colleagues' warnings about the company's instability and insanity. And the 14-hour days, salvaging underbid contracts, and dealing with irritating clients and colleagues, exacted a toll. She'd stagger home exhausted and tried sleeping in the late afternoons, but even while she slept, anxiety stabbed her awake.

Pulling into the parking spot, Zara surveyed the fifteen-story, soulless glass tower. "Thing looks like a charred dick. How symbolic," she thought, while rifling through the back of her RAV4 for her portfolios. "Could this be any more purposeless?"

THE INTERIOR RESEMBLED every other newer office building in Minneapolis, with the prerequisite convenience store, dry cleaner, Caribou Coffee, and Brian Z's deli. Fake brick and lots of windows guaranteed the offices were too cold in the winter. During summer, the glass magnified the sun's rays, slowly roasting its occupants.

Zara opened the glass door and noticed Miss Mary, the receptionist, was on a call. She scurried past her, hoping to avoid a conversation.

"Good morning, Zara!" said Miss Mary, slamming the phone. Eighty-year-old Mary was the owner's mother, and quite the sight. With pink dandelion puff-ball hair, she resembled Barbara Cartland (sans jewels and furs) and spent her days behind an oversized oak veneer desk, swapping recipes, gossip, and doing occasional work-related tasks.

"Hey, Mary," said Zara, zipping past her.

"Zara," said Miss Mary, calling after her, "Do you have a recipe for quiche?"

"Uh, no," said Zara through gritted teeth. "Remember? I don't cook, bake, or do any of that stuff!"

"Oh," said Miss Mary, sounding dejected.

Walking down the long row of cubicles to her office, Zara got a whiff of pot and glanced over at Joel, one of the designers, gazing intently at his monitor, watching the screen saver as it painted rainbows.

At least this is better than last month when he OD'd on coke and ecstasy right before lunch. Zara had never seen anyone have a seizure until that day.

Zara was counting the days until Elly's return. Zara came to work for this company because of Elly. For ten years, they'd been in each other's lives, first as mentor/mentee, then colleagues—but always friends. Zara wanted to tell Elly about Pearl, Aunt Martha, and the *Eastland*. Elly would understand, maybe even better than Zara did.

Zara saw other coworkers standing around in the aisles.

"Hey, Zara," said Scott, a blond man in his early twenties who was a designer. "We're going to the Mall for drinks and late-night bowling. Want to come?"

"Thanks, Scott, but I have plans tonight," said Zara.

"Plans, did I hear you say you have plans?" said Polly, who was one of the project coordinators.

"Yes. Plans!" said Zara.

"Do tell," said Polly, following Zara inside her office and closing the door. Polly, about 45 years old, was wedged into a pair of bib overalls. She resembled Pippi Longstocking—the later years—with freckles and orange-red pigtails.

"Nothing to tell," said Zara, opening the door. She hoped Polly would leave, but even when Zara tried, Polly refused to be insulted.

"Come on! Who is she? Who is the next Mrs. Vrabel?" said Polly.

"Knock it off, Polly! I'm doing some research, that's all," said Zara.

"If you say so," said Polly, winking and walking away.

Closing her door, Zara logged onto her computer, stared at the fifteen "urgent" emails, and turned away.

Taking a legal pad from her desk, she jotted down:

Martha Pfeiffer. Born November 13, 1895, Johnstown, PA. Died July 24, 1915, Chicago, IL.

Whatever happened between those dates? What happened on the day of the Eastland Disaster?

Zara had no clue how to solve this mystery, but tomorrow was Saturday, and she could carry on. She had no time to waste.

The Library, the Store and More

On Saturday, Zara awakened at 3:00 a.m. and began reviewing her notes from the call with Aunt Pearl. Studying her decrepit PC and antiquated modem, she could now justify replacing them—she needed a powerful machine to embark on this magnificent quest.

True, she could research at work, but more often than not, the network was down. Manfred, the network administrator, had his own reliability issues since returning from his two-month stay at Hazelden. Although he wasn't blacking out and accidentally setting the computer room on fire, he wasn't eager to solve network problems. So, when Zara once asked when the network would be up and running, he smiled and said, "One day at a time."

Time for technological self-sufficiency.

On the way to CompUSA, she stopped at the Roseville Library, where they had recently added a Dunn Brothers Coffee shop.

"Love that library," she said, sipping a latte. She watched the coffee roaster spinning round and round, trying to catch up with what was happening to her.

When the library opened, she beelined toward a terminal. Under the *Subject keywords,* she typed and entered "Eastland." Nothing displayed—other than a page of authors with the last name of "Eastman."

Next, she tried "Shipping Disasters," which had some promising results.

Rifling through the stacks, she found books with titles such as *Great Ships of the Great Lakes* and learned of many shipping disasters, such as the *Lady Elgin,* whose name popped up in multiple places. Zara thumbed through the most recent book, written in 1973, which devoted three sentences to the *Eastland* Disaster.

Frustrated, she left the library and drove a mile down the road to

CompUSA, where she plunked down $1100 for a new Compaq PC. State-of-the-art: 350 MHz, 128 RAM, 20 GB hard drive, and 32X CD-ROM. Upon returning to her apartment, she spent Saturday afternoon setting it up and getting the modem to connect. After multiple calls to tech support, everything was working—for the moment.

Elly wouldn't return until late Sunday and, while Zara couldn't wait to speak with her, she also didn't want to inundate her. Elly would be drained after working all week in New York City. Still, Zara left a message on Elly's machine, saying, "Welcome back! Have we got to talk! See you soon."

~

ZARA'S PHONE rang at 6:00 a.m. on Monday.

"Zee-Girl," said the chirpy voice on the other end.

"Elly!!! When did you get back?"

"Oh, please," said Elly. "I should have known better than let Miss Mary book the flight—the plane wasn't there, and no one seemed to know where to find it!"

"What'd she book you on?"

"Vanguard. Apparently, they only own seven planes, so I can see how easy it would be to misplace one. I made a stink and finally got put on a plane, but had to get to Minneapolis via Charlotte, and maybe Atlanta. I lost track."

"Nothing like an unexpected tour of the southeastern United States."

"I got in about 2:00 a.m. and was so wired, I couldn't sleep—I almost called you! As much as I love traveling, I hated being gone so long. Thanks for taking care of Giovanni and Anna Magnani."

"No problem! I consider them my step-cats, y'know."

"Tell you what—I have to run some errands and should be done around 11:30. God knows I want to delay getting into the office. Why don't we meet for lunch at Taste of Thailand first?"

Elly

"There you are!" screamed Zara, running over to the dark-haired woman seated at the small table for two.

The Taste of Thailand, housed in a former Happy Chef restaurant on the bustling and heavily trafficked Lyndale Avenue, was their favorite lunch spot.

Eleanore D'Angelo epitomized zaftig: dark, boisterous, and buxom. Impeccably attired with matching crimson lipstick, nails, dress, and heels, Elly resembled Connie Francis, to whom she claimed to be a distant relative.

With minimal makeup, spiked blonde hair, swimmer's build, high-top tennis shoes, and cargo pants, Zara contrasted strikingly with Elly, so much so that Elly, just five years older, was sometimes mistaken for Zara's mother. Once, when they were out, the server asked Elly what her "daughter" would have. Without missing a beat, Elly said, "A Shirley Temple for my little girl."

Although mismatched on the surface, the two were otherwise simpatico. Zara once told Elly, "Whatever I've lacked in romantic relationships, I've had great friends, especially you!"

Elly concurred, "I'm so off men, I used to wish I could somehow be a lesbian—but after listening to your tales of woe, I thought, it's no better where you are! But I sure love having you as my friend."

They hugged and discussed Elly's trip.

"It went well," said Elly.

"How could it not, Elly? I mean, you're the best stand-up trainer we have—audiences love you!" said Zara.

"Yeah," said Elly, sighing.

"What's the matter?" said Zara.

"I'm anxious about our company—I think they're playing fast and loose with the books again. Christ! I should have stayed independent and not given into Stevie's begging me to work for them. And I feel responsible for dragging you in."

"Hey, I'm a big girl," said Zara. "Well, I'm not surprised by those low-lifes. In fact, I'm convinced they have made a pact with Satan."

"But they're all born-again, speaking-in-tongues believers!" said Elly, with a wink. "That's another thing. Why is Stevie hiring so many people from his dad's megachurch? None of them have any real qualifications for anything except selling Herbal-glow or whatever that's called. Isn't that illegal?"

"Why would that be any different from the other sleazy stuff they get into? If we wrote a book about this outfit, no one would believe it," said Zara, rocking back and forth on her chair, reading the Chinese horoscopes on the placemat.

"That's for sure," said Elly, inspecting her newly arrived order of drunken noodles.

"This is the only company where management has prayer meetings in the morning and spends the afternoon locked in their offices viewing porn on the 'net,'" said Elly. "And there was that 'incident' with Stevie and his former secretary! How do you think we ended up with Stevie's mother as the receptionist?"

"Well, I think the PTL Club set a precedent along those lines," said Zara, drinking her ginseng tea. "Ish! This stuff is horrible, and I don't care how damn healthy it's supposed to be. I would like to order some plum wine. Care to join me?"

"Isn't there some company rule that you can't drink during business hours?" said Elly.

"That's right, you can spend hours looking at porn, but no drinking. Hell, Russ, Stevie, and Bjorn are probably locked in their offices doing God knows what," said Zara.

"True enough," said Elly. "Flag down the waitperson, and let's get a carafe."

"Now you're talking," said Zara.

"Tell me your news. What have you been up to? I felt like I was gone for a year, not a week. Whew, I'm always relieved when those seminars are over, even if they're in New York. Too tired to have fun at night! So, who are you dating this week?" said Elly.

"Well, I was seeing those three women—not all at once, mind you —but I'm not seeing anyone now," said Zara.

"What is going on?!" said Elly. "I've never known you not to have someone. You've always said it was always good to have a few irons in the fire?"

"Words to live by," said Zara. "But not now. I'm working on something, and it's taking a lot of time and energy."

"What? Another woman?" said Elly.

"In a way," said Zara.

"Tell me!" said Elly.

"I promise I will, but not yet," said Zara. "It's kind of weird."

"I will hold you to that! I want to meet your mystery woman," said Elly.

"Me, too," said Zara.

"Huh?" said Elly.

"I'll explain later," said Zara.

~

RETURNING to work at 1:30 p.m., Zara and Elly slipped into their shared office.

"What did I tell you, El! Every door closed," said Zara, shaking her head. "Say, would you mind if I made a few phone calls? I have to talk to the Dearborn folks to see how the project is going."

"No prob," said Elly, gathering papers. "I have to dig out my mess. Yuk. They sure piled on the work while I was gone."

Zara began dialing.

"Son-of-a-bitch!" said Zara, slamming the receiver.

"What?" said Elly.

"Those morons didn't pay the damn long-distance bill again! I can't call out!" said Zara.

"Again?" said Elly.

"Dammit to hell, all of my clients are out-of-state, and I can't talk to them!" said Zara.

"Didn't they give you a cell phone?" said Elly.

"Yeah, but they didn't pay that bill, either," said Zara.

"What's amazing is that they'll blame you for this," said Elly.

"Last week, it was the casting agent—I was trying to hire talent for the Scanlon industrial. Do you know that Sally Morton won't work with us anymore unless we pay upfront? Our company has such a terrible reputation for nonpayment, and Sally was tired of getting burned. So, I couldn't cast my commercial," said Zara.

"Why don't you talk to Stevie?" said Elly.

"I have. You know Stevie, 'I'll get on that right away,' and then nothing. I'm getting heart palpitations again, and I'm too young to croak," said Zara. "Time for a new job."

"Your heart's acting up? You better get back to that cardiologist," said Elly.

"She'll tell me the same thing she said before—get a less-stressful job," said Zara.

"This isn't stress. It's a goddamn death march. It's Russian roulette," said Elly.

"Should we start another company?" said Zara.

"Only if it's just us. Talk about a heart attack waiting to happen," said Elly. "I never want to go through what we went through at Quest Productions!"

"Well, the embezzling bookkeeper didn't help, I know, but that was the late 80s. It's the late 90s now, and this dot-com thing is taking off. Could be promising," said Zara.

"I will consider it. At least we paid our bills, unlike this place," said Elly. "Well, the hell with these scripts. I'm going to pack up this crap and leave for the day. I work better at home, anyway. How about you?"

"There are a few things I want to do, like update my resume and do some job hunting," said Zara.

"What about your new computer?" said Elly.

"Well, I just got it set up, and still need to stabilize the internet connection. I'm gonna get a different cable from Manfred's box of computer junk. God, I better make sure I take all my personal stuff home, too," said Zara.

"Why?" said Elly.

"I have this recurring nightmare where the office doors are chained and bolted. Do they even pay the rent on these suites?" said Zara.

"Whoa. You could be right. Well, don't stay long. Forget about this joint and have a good evening," said Elly.

"You, too, El. See you, mañana," said Zara, watching Elly walk down the hall.

Sitting at her computer, Zara first wanted to search for companies hiring producers or scriptwriters but paused.

Instead, she typed *Eastland* into the search field, clicked *go*, and closed her eyes. When she opened them, she got what she expected —next to nothing—except links to towns, high schools, and a shoe company called Eastland. This time, though, something told her to keep scrolling, and so she did. Then, there it was—the last entry at the bottom of the page.

Eastland Disaster of 1915 - the steamer *Eastland* sank in the Chicago River in 1915, killing 844 employees of the Western Electric Company

"Oh, my God!" said Zara, covering her mouth with both hands.

The link opened a new page with a panoramic view of the humongous ship lying on its side in the Chicago River, sandwiched between warehouses and docks. People, like ants, were everywhere. Some were astride the massive hulk, drilling and burning holes into its side with blowtorches. Others were yanking bodies from the ship's hull, playing to an audience of hundreds standing on the docks.

The inscription on the bottom of the photo, "The Wreck of the *Eastland*," took Zara's breath away. Turning away, she stared at the wall, while "The Wreck of the Edmund Fitzgerald" blasted in her head.

"My God. I found it and this is it! It's really real!"

Gazing at the ship's photo for several minutes, she clicked

another link, which opened a page of more images. She was light-headed and nauseous and put her head between her legs, hoping she wouldn't retch.

Oh, dearest Martha. You should have gone on to more picnics, more outfits, friends, and hats and not this wretched end. How could this be forgotten? I don't know how, but I promise I will change that.

She went home.

ZARA PITCHED her backpack on the couch and dashed to her bedroom office. She powered on her new computer and hoped the modem would behave. Then, locating the *Eastland* website again, she skipped the images and began printing out the narratives.

She emailed the website's owner, Ellen. While she had no personal connection to the *Eastland*, Ellen loved Great Lakes' shipping disasters. She bought most of the cards and photos from antique shops, scanned them and uploaded them to her website.

Jotting notes from the website, and breaking numerous pencil leads, Zara composed her own account. Pressing the words into paper made it real.

Eastland Disaster notes

On early Saturday morning, July 24, 1915, in downtown Chicago, between Clark and LaSalle Street, thousands of people waited to board one of the six large ships that Western Electric had chartered for its annual picnic on Lake Michigan.

Demographics: most were Western Electric employees, their families, and friends. Many were Italian, Eastern European, or Central European immigrants—or children of immigrants—between 16 and 21 years old.

About two thousand boarded the *Eastland*. Shortly after boarding, the ship began listing (leaning) starboard (toward the dock). As the listing increased, the ship's chief engineer ordered the port ballast tanks to be filled enough to help steady the liner. That seemed to do the trick for a few minutes. However, the ship again listed—this time in the other direction. As the passengers kept boarding, the vessel became increasingly unsteady. The engineering crew emptied the ballast tanks to straighten out the list.

By this time, the gangplank closed, and most of the 2,500 passengers had settled on the port side. The list continued, reaching a 30-degree angle, and water started gushing into the ship. Tables, chairs, picnic baskets, and other items propelled across the decks. As furnishings and appliances crashed around them, passengers began scrambling.

The listing continued until the ship tipped over on its side. Some who fell overboard treaded water, while hundreds of others were trapped inside or underneath the ship.

One eyewitness recounted hearing the shrieking of those trapped inside the ship. By the time rescue workers had cut holes in the hull's side, the screaming had ceased. Many inside were injured or had died.

The captain and the crew escaped. To top it off, the captain tried to prevent rescuers from torching holes in the ship's side!

That afternoon, an armory had been converted to serve as the central morgue for all of the bodies. The horses dutifully hauled bodies through the July heat until some of them collapsed and gave up the ghost in their ultimate act of faithful service.

The bodies were laid out in rows inside the morgue. Later that evening, family members arrived to identify their loved ones.

ZARA LEARNED THE UNTHINKABLE: like the Johnstown Flood, the *Eastland* Disaster was preventable.

From the time it was constructed (1903), several incidents led many to claim the *Eastland* was unsafe because of its top-heaviness. During an excursion in 1903, passengers reported the listing problem.

Yet, the issue was never corrected, and the ship passed federal inspection.

The additional lifeboats added (in response to the *Titanic*) contributed to the *Eastland's* instability. After the 1915 catastrophe, the *Eastland* was restored and renamed as the USS Wilmette. It served as a training vessel for the Illinois Naval Reserve until its decommissioning in 1945.

The secret of the *Eastland's* obliteration from history lay buried deep in Chicago's consciousness. Why was the *Eastland* not given equal footing with the Great Fire, where far fewer people had died? [1]

Why would Chicago forget its own Titanic?

Did the ripples from her Aunt Martha's death continue flowing through her grandmother's life, her mother's life, and now finally into hers?

Could someone inherit more than just eye and hair color from their direct—and even indirect—ancestors? What about memories? If so, why was it so pronounced in her life? Of all people, Zara could have been voted "least likely to care about family history" if there was such a thing.

Why did her mother or sister not feel the connection?

The ghost stories Magda told her were entertaining, but Zara, like her mother, grew to be skeptical. Her mother said, "Superstition is an easy way to avoid actual thinking."

ZARA PULLED ANOTHER ALL-NIGHTER, reading and re-examining the narratives, and the photos. She couldn't stop looking at the images of limp, dripping bodies extricated out of the side of the ship.

Forever seared in her mind was the ominous image of the *Eastland* serenely and absurdly resting on its side, while entombing hundreds of bodies. This now belonged to her, and she wondered what to do with it.

Sweat beads trickled down her face, while Zara rubbed the space in between her eyes as if it were Aladdin's lamp, hoping for enlightenment. By 3:30 a.m., Zara simultaneously focused on everything—and nothing. Lying in bed, she stared at the ceiling.

I wonder if I'll ever be able to sleep again?

I don't know what's enraging me more—that this thing was preventable, that my great-aunt died, or that I didn't know about it until now! How fair is this?

Years ago, she relinquished hope of discovering anything unusual about her mother's family and wrote them off. And now, midway through her own life, her Great-Aunt Martha emerges from a shipwreck.

Zara wondered what was wrong with Martha's surviving brothers and sisters. Did they ever contact her mother when their sister, Zara's grandmother, passed away at such a young age, leaving a baby behind?

MORNING CAME TOO SOON, but instead of rushing to the office, Zara planted herself at the kitchen table again.

Why is this so hard? Why am I rattled to the core? This event and this woman are so intimately bonded to me, yet so out of reach.

There must be some explanation.

Her emotions ran wild and in multiple directions—inhaling glee and exhaling despair.

ZARA LATER CALLED her mother to tell her about Pearl, the *Eastland*, and Aunt Martha. She was never sure what type of reception she'd get and prepared for the worst.

"What do you think, Mom?" said Zara.

"I don't know what to think," said Helena. "When I was a kid, I went to Chicago for the first—and only—time to visit Pearl."

"Didn't you talk about this stuff? About family history?" said Zara.

"Pearl was thirteen years older than I was and, for all intents and purposes, was a stranger," said her mom. "Traveling over 500 miles back then wasn't easy. When I met her for the first time, she was about thirty years old and married—they had just adopted baby Johnny. She told me about a 'ferry boat disaster' where my mother's sister was killed, but I wasn't interested. I was a kid. I never knew my mother and was just getting to know my half-sister, so it seemed unreal."

"So, what's it like learning this?"

"I don't know what to think," repeated Helena. "There's so much I never knew."

ZARA DIDN'T WANT to share Aunt Martha with anyone outside of her family, since it was so new and fragile, but she'd burst if she couldn't tell Elly.

Elly was on calls but would see Zara after work. Zara walked over to Elly's home, a cozy bungalow across from Zara's alma mater, Martin Luther Seminary, and about a mile west of Zara's apartment.

Elly's home reflected its owner—shabby chic. She bought everything—from furniture to artwork—at estate sales and antique shops and decorated with style. She chose cream and off-white colors for her couch covers and chairs, while opting for periwinkle blue bookshelves.

They sat at Elly's weather worn kitchen table while Zara filled her in.

"The *Eastland*, huh? I'm Chicago, born and bred, and never heard of it," said Elly.

"No one's heard of it. At least that's how it seems. I suspect the internet will change that, but until then, it's like it never happened," said Zara.

"Family secrets carried to the extreme. Well, regardless, Zara, this is fantastically huge! You've been carrying all this around and have told no one. That's not like you."

"None of this is like me. It's like I'm on some unknown path where

I'm totally lost. But occasionally, I feel there's light straight ahead, and I have to keep walking. Make sense?"

"No. Yet, it seems right."

"I haven't felt this disoriented since my dad died. My great-aunt seems to be calling out to me. Is that possible? Why bother with me —with someone so disconnected from most of their family?"

"Maybe because you weren't looking."

"Huh?"

"If you're desperately seeking a relationship, you never find it. But then, when you've made peace with it, and are content to be single for the rest of your days, that's when—bang!—you meet that special person. Maybe it's like that, but only it's your family this time. You gave up on needing them and their approval long ago. You moved on, and now, here you are, back at square one."

"I don't know," said Zara.

Elly continued, "Or maybe you're the only one who could hear her. I mean, don't you have some witches and psychics in your family?"

"Yeah, but Aunt Magda is the only one who would admit it," said Zara.

"Could you talk to her about it?" said Elly.

"Maybe if we had a séance, since she died five years ago," said Zara.

"Too bad, but time to step up to the plate," said Elly.

"No way in hell. Even if I have that kind of gift—which I hope I don't—I'd want to trade it in for something else. A Porsche maybe," said Zara.

"Why wouldn't you want it? Mediums and psychics are very popular," said Elly. "Think of it! You could have a TV show. Talking to the dead is big money."

"If I learned anything from Aunt Magda, it's that, unless you're fond of three-ring circuses, you don't tell people about those abilities. Magda was swarmed by people coming to her door at all hours of the day and night!"

"Did you believe she could talk to the dead?"

"No. But she believed it, and I respected her. She was wise and extremely good at reading people."

"Intuitive," said Elly.

"Yes," said Zara. "But what is intuition, except the ability to bypass the five senses and still get something right?"

"So, you admit that intuition might be a real thing?" said Elly.

"Well, yes. I mean, today's superstition can be tomorrow's science, right?" said Zara.

"This is some secret project, my girl! And all this time, I thought you were carrying on another clandestine love affair. This is a helluva lot more substantial than your usual," said Elly.

"Damn it, El! You think I'm a superficial womanizer?"

"Ooh, getting testy, are we? Well, no one, dearest Zara, would call you superficial," said Elly.

Zara glared at Elly, but then started laughing.

"I've known you for what—a thousand years—and you've always been running around. Sometimes I envied your freedom, but I also wondered about you. You're so steady in every other aspect of life— fiercely independent and unafraid of being alone. What were you running from?" said Elly.

Zara touched her chin and paused. "I dunno. This experience— it's thrown me into quest mode. I don't think I've ever felt that in my life."

"How about that religious community in Detroit, or at the seminary?" asked Elly.

"Detroit was about changing myself and the world—if I had time. I was just 19—Martha's age—when I joined that merry little cult. And seminary was a last-ditch effort to salvage something from my Lutheran roots."

"You have done some unusual things."

"But this isn't like anything else I've ever done, Elly, because I don't know what I'm walking into."

"What's scary?" asked Elly.

"I thought I was done with these friggin' vision quest thingys, but now I have answers to questions that I stopped asking years ago," said Zara.

"Is it kind of like being adopted? Your perpetual restlessness—always looking for something. Forever the outsider. And now you meet your long-lost family, and you're reeling," said Elly.

"That's as good a metaphor as any!"

"I love an excellent metaphor! But seriously, Zee, take time for this. It probably has been brewing beneath the surface your entire life. It's like that movie, *Magnificent Obsession*," said Elly.

"I don't remember the movie, but I like the title," said Zara. "There's something else that's coming up. Something that I don't like."

"What's that?"

"Regrets. I have more than a few. What kind of writer am I? Why didn't I question my mom about her family when I was younger instead of dismissing them! Maybe, I would have understood my family much better and would have been slower to judge them —and me."

"This is stirring the broody melancholic Slavic blood in your veins," laughed Elly. "Look! Most kids rebel against their families when they're young. It's a rite of passage. And later, when they're middle-aged, they appreciate that which they rejected. You're not that unique, dearie."

"I suppose," said Zara.

"And before you rip yourself to shreds, consider this: given the time and circumstances under which you grew up, rebelling was your only choice."

"Suppose."

"Some of your family members weren't very nice to you. If you'd stayed, you may have ended up in a terrible place. Tell me how you could have come out of the closet in Cleveland surrounded by all those judgmental relatives? Huh? You had the guts to leave every-thing you knew and go West—well, Midwest anyway."

"I'm listening," said Zara

"We've reached the end of my wisdom for the moment. I love my self-help books, but I don't have any that talk about coping with dead relatives."

"Too bad. I'd love to have a roadmap for this voyage."

"You don't need one. They have your attention now and you'll probably get stronger directional inclinations if that's an actual thing."

"If this doesn't kill me first," said Zara.

"What are you talking about?" said Elly.

"I feel I'm being absorbed into a vortex, so maybe your magnificent obsession idea is right. This furtive, futile yearning is eating me alive. I don't want to just read about Martha—I want to go back into her past and meet her."

"Look, you have information overload right now. Let the dust settle. Do what you do best—write. It will help make sense of it."

"Elly, I hope you're right."

JUST AS ZARA was in the midst of her Eastland Disaster research, another *Titanic* movie was released. She could not escape "My Heart Will Go On," which seemed to play whenever she turned on the radio. She was disgusted. The *Titanic* has yet another celluloid tribute, and only a handful of people knew of the *Eastland*.

"Their deaths were of no consequence to anyone save their families and employers," wrote George Hilton.[2] Zara finally found Hilton's definitive book about the *Eastland*, a tome weighed down by facts, figures and dry narrative. It was a good reference but provided no comfort or insight.

And the *Titanic* stuck in her craw. The *Eastland* Disaster was also an epic scandal. A ship of immigrants, and immigrants' children, capsizing in a harbor in downtown Chicago didn't rate as highly as a large luxury liner filled with big names careening into an iceberg.

How does a city, much less a country, forget 844 lives snuffed out in a day? Very selective, who gets remembered, and what gets forgotten. But sometimes, what's forgotten has the most power. Whatever the reason for this curious collective amnesia, Zara wanted it in people's consciousness.

With all the bizarre debacles and tragedies under its historical belt, Chicago should have awarded the *Eastland* a perverted claim to fame.

6

SKETCHING AN UN-LIVED LIFE

Elly was right—it was time to write about Martha, and Zara had a guaranteed spot for the article. She rang the *Bugle's* editor.

"Go for it, Zara! Sounds fantastic," he said. "Just get it to us right after Labor Day."

Still, she only had a sparse narrative and wasn't sure how to proceed. Pearl had recently sent additional photos that she'd hope would provide inspiration. As she lined them up on her living room coffee table, she watched Martha evolve.

By age five, Martha was adorable, sporting an oversized bow and smiling eyes. At age 12, standing next to her sister Luisa, she was still cute, but something else was going on. She stood erect, hand on hip, and gazed into the camera as if she was daring it to break contact first. She appeared to be gauging her surroundings, unsure if she could rely on them totally. Zara shuddered. This was eerily similar to many of her own childhood photos.

Still, by her late teens, Martha was posing, growing into her beauty, and possessing a flair for style.

And then, there it was. The last picture, taken during her final year, featuring Martha flanked by several young women—all of whom wore men's clothing. By then, Martha appeared no longer innocent.

In this case, a picture is not always worth a thousand words. Especially this one. *What was the cross-dressing about, Aunt Martha?*

WHAT DO I carry of you inside my veins? And how do I bring you into my life?

As a writer, Zara was known for capturing her subject's unique imprint upon their world in 1,000 words or less (word count limits for most publications).

After winning first place for commentaries in the Annual Community Newspaper Association's "Best of" competition, one judge wrote, "It's as if you sculpt with words."

Writing about strangers was easy. Family? Not so easy. Could she do it?

CONSTRUCTING a plausible narrative from shards and fragments torpedoed her confidence.

How can I write about a family I'd never known, and a time and a city in which I'd never lived?

Still, this story was bequeathed to her, and she must render it with her usual style.

Something was at stake—but what? Her life? Her family's life? The past? The future? The phrase *Make it yours* echoed in her head.

Who are you, Martha Pfeiffer, and what do you want from me?

Zara pieced sentences together, and things clicked. Words flowed and fit into their places on the page, and the momentum intensified.

The story's voltage flooded her being and after a few fits and starts, she crafted an exceptional essay about Martha and the *Eastland*.

This is damn good! Damn good. Oh, maybe it's not. The ending is kind of clunky!

She rang Elly.

"Hey, can we get together to look at my article?"

"Are you kidding? I love being needed, particularly when it's you who needs me. Give me ten minutes, and I'll be over."

Elly's need to be useful baffled Zara, who had no such inclination.

Zara gazed at Elly, who was nearly face down in the article.

When she finally looked up, Elly said, "This is your best one yet. Here's what I've always loved about your writing: besides the fact that you can actually write, you're very generous. You always let your subject's voice come through. You get out of the way and let them shine—even in a case like this where your subject is dead. But..."

"What? Stop blathering!" said Zara defensively.

"Don't bark at me! You know what! That ending is forced! It flows lyrically, wafting toward the clouds, and suddenly crash-lands! It's like you got scared and ran away!" said Elly, sipping her tea. "You know what? Go to Chicago to see Martha's world. At least see her grave—you must see her ending to write a real ending. *Capisce?* Otherwise, you leave your reader hanging. Just like you are."

"Nothing like a grave to bring one back to earth," said Zara.

"I'm serious! Martha's taking on mythic proportions, and you can't live an isolated life with a ghost. Go to Chicago."

"Chicago's at least an eight-hour drive, and I don't know even know where Bethania Cemetery is," said Zara.

"When's the article due?"

"The Wednesday after Labor Day."

"Well, Labor Day weekend is coming up, so you'll have time to drive to Chicago. Stay with your Aunt Pearl. You're having fun getting to know her, and she'd probably enjoy the company."

"Not this time. I want to see Pearl, but not when I'm working on an article. When I'm writing, I'm not the most hospitable character on the planet," said Zara.

"True. You'd make a lousy first impression," said Elly. "Stay somewhere between the Cities and Chicago to break up the drive. How about La Crosse? It's not exactly halfway, but it's pretty, with the river and the old downtown area. School won't be in session, so it should be quiet."

"Yeah, that could work," said Zara. "Can you come with me, El? You know how bad I am at directions. And Chicago!? It scares the shit out of me. And what if the cemetery is in some godforsaken place?"

"Uh-uh, chick! Some other time, I promise."

"Please!"

"You need to fly solo for this one. Don't worry. We'll get a detailed map. Besides, I think you're wrong. She's not buried in Chicago proper, but in some 'burb, what's it called?"

"Justice? Some name, huh?" said Zara.

"Justice!" said Elly, snapping her finger. "Of course!"

"You know where it is?" said Zara.

"Yes! Bethania's next to Resurrection Cemetery—the home of Resurrection Mary!"

"Who?" said Zara.

"Haven't you ever heard of Chicago's most famous hitchhiking ghost?" said Elly.

"No," said Zara. "Why's she called Resurrection Mary?"

"She's the ghostly hitchhiker who always wants to be driven to Resurrection Cemetery. A driver picks her up, goes down Archer Avenue past Resurrection Cemetery, and, just like that, she vanishes. Lots of people have given her rides through the years. Well, anyway, Resurrection Cemetery and Bethania share the same area. You'll be right at home—it's just one long cemetery," said Elly.

"Umm, do you believe it?" said Zara.

"What? Resurrection Mary? I dunno, but let's say I have an open mind," said Elly, walking over to the computer. "Let's get online and make hotel reservations, and we'll get directions to Justice."

"I'll give Resurrection Mary your regards."

DEATH SETS *a Thing Significant*[1]

—*Emily Dickinson.*

Zara had to see and touch Martha's grave—she needed hard evidence.

Sometimes I think I know you, but I don't want to make you over in my image, as tempting as that is. Who are you, Martha Pfeiffer, and why are you taking over my life?

～

THE EVENING before her Chicago trip, Zara met Elly at Muffuletta restaurant. Elly already ordered red wine, French bread, and roasted garlic.

"We have to celebrate this occasion," said Elly.

"I feel as if I'm going to see Martha," said Zara. "You think I'm nuts, don't you? Well, even if you don't, I do."

"I've always seen you as courageous and no-nonsense. Someone who didn't give a damn about what others thought because you were true to yourself. You've lived life on your own terms, so why are you worried about appearing crazy?"

"I get scared that maybe I'll end up like my dad," she said.

"Stop it! Your dad had severe trauma in his life. There was no help available, and it caught up to him, that's all. There's nothing wrong with you," said Elly.

"I feel so damn vulnerable, and I don't do vulnerable," said Zara, mashing a garlic clove into her bread slice.

"Ahh, you're afraid she won't be there for you," said Elly.

"I feel like that guy in the movie, *Laura*. He falls for a portrait of a dead woman, except that his dead woman turned up alive. Mine won't," said Zara.

"Brings up the family outcast role that you've played since forever. Give that up. You're just like them—like her. Maybe she was assigned to watch over you. Mama always said we had at least one guardian angel."

"My Aunt Magda did, too,"

"Nothing wrong with wanting a heart connection to someone in your family. Nothing wrong with wanting to be loved by your blood. Finding that, with a dead relative, will be tricky, but not impossible," said Elly.

Tears flooded Zara's eyes. "But Elly! It's wonderful, and yet I'm homesick for a place and time that I never lived. I feel lost."

"When this is done, you will have accomplished something tremendous. You are officially now the connective tissue in this family. Yeah! You, ya little pariah!"

Zara started laughing.

"You're bringing your living family to their history. Your mother never knew her mother's family, and you gave that precious gift to her. You've already given Aunt Pearl what every writer wants—to know their writing changed someone's life! As for your sister, it might not mean much to her now, but down the road, it will. For you? A new chapter is about to begin."

"El, you're fantastic," said Zara, taking her friend's hand.

"I'm psychic in my own way, too," laughed Elly. "Mama said I was born with a caul on my head—to Sicilians, that meant you were born with the sixth sense. Then, there's my last name. D'Angelo—of the angels."

"You're pretty good, El. I will say that," said Zara.

"Let's pay the bill and get out of here. You have a long drive to La Crosse tomorrow, and I have two codependent cats waiting," said Elly.

"And Z-girl, go crazy! Make up every fantastic story you can about Martha. You'll feel better, I'll feel better, and you'll have the strong closer for your piece."

"Jumpstart me," said Zara. "I mean, your training icebreakers are legendary!"

"Okay. Here's the scene. You haven't seen your Aunt Martha since you were four years old, and you're coming to visit her now. So get past the niceties and ask her what kind of finale she wants for the article. See what she says," said Elly.

"Brilliant! I can take it from there," said Zara.

Saturday, Labor Day Weekend, September 5, 1998, 4:00 a.m.

Traveling down Highway 61 in Minnesota, Zara was hedged in by the mighty Mississippi River to the left and slab-like rock formations to the right. She reveled in dawn's creamy orange sun, cloudless skies, and the empty, curving two-lane highway.

She visualized meeting Aunt Martha for the first time. Stopped and restarted the scene, changing the dialogue each time. What would she say if she could see and talk with Martha? What *could* she say? Would she be ecstatic, or resent Martha's premature departure and dramatic comeback?

The two-and-a-half hours to La Crosse gave time for uncertainty, too.

How can I be sure of something that can't be? Magda's stories enchanted me when I was a child, but later, I replaced enchantment with doubt. Lots of doubt. Appearing sophisticated and erudite was more important.

I don't believe in life after death. Not really. A dead relative—someone I never met—is communicating with me? This is impossible. The only problem is that it's happening.

Thinking of her family and her strained, strange relationship with them, she alternated between feeling embarrassed and amused at her long-ago tirades. As a ten-year-old, she named herself the Changeling, declaring that she was the master of her fate. Those proclamations were born in the heart of a sensitive child who wondered why certain family members seemed to hate her. While no longer a child, she was still susceptible to rejection.

Zara longed for her twenty-year-old self. In the early seventies, that girl boarded a bus bound for communal living in an inner-city Detroit alternative religious community. Ahh, the seventies. She valued "calling" over calculating risk then. She loved that crazy kid.

Where'd you go, kid? Are you in there somewhere?

The alternative religious community offered quite a package deal. If you joined, they promised to cure your flaws, give you meaning, and discern God's will—since you were incapable of doing that on your own. In addition, the all-male leadership offered many young women members various unconventional therapeutic methods to "heal" them. What did they need "healing" from? She never knew. Zara shuddered and kiboshed those thoughts before they gained a foothold.

Although she never fell for the grift, she helplessly watched other young women starve themselves to please the central leader. And the "chosen" ones would enter into a special relationship with this guy and his minions.

Zara was immune to lecherous and lascivious males, thinking of them as pesky insects needing squashing. But, while she wasn't looking, she ran headlong into her true self. Four years there could not inoculate her against who she was. Then, despite her genuine efforts to resist the flesh, she met a woman. A married woman. And that was a royal, bloody mess, culminating in a witch hunt. Other community leaders, most of whom were carrying on extramarital heterosexual relationships, threw Zara and this woman into a circle each morning and cast out "demons." It was brutal.

Zara countered by lambasting the elders, reciting a detailed litany of each one's various transgressions—she'd been tracking their B.S. in her hidden notebook for a while. After that, the self-anointed ones backed down and offered Zara her heart's desire. For the first time, she witnessed the blatant, unadulterated hypocrisy and sadism of good religious folk. The experience was a death blow to her faith. She walked away and returned to her family in Ohio. The married woman returned to her husband in England, blamed Zara for everything, and vanished forever from the stage of Zara's life, leaving her shattered and heartbroken. She was just 22.

Zara seldom let her guard down afterward. In her late twenties, she embraced the rebel role. The years of distancing herself formed a chasm between her and the rest of the world. Could she ever trust anyone?

Although she did not lack friends, like Elly, or lovers, something was missing. And now, she desperately needed a particular someone in her family.

If you could have been there when I was a kid, you could have helped me! She shouted, hoping Martha would awaken from her eternal slumber.

Driving around the bend at Lake Pepin, Zara noticed a few boats on the water, getting in some early morning sailing and water-skiing, and she suddenly ached for mindless fun.

Regardless of the weekend's outcome, Zara would end up with a complete story. An exceptional tale of a young woman—a part of her family, a part of her—who lived briefly and then perished violently.

∾

La Crosse, Wisconsin

Around 9:30 a.m., she pulled up to the Courtyard Suites parking lot in La Crosse. Too early to check-in, so Zara had breakfast in their restaurant. Although Labor Day weekends can grow cold in the upper Midwest, this one was unusually balmy. Seeing nothing but gentle waves and a lone paddleboat on the river calmed her.

She didn't realize how fatigued she was until that moment and wasn't up to challenging herself. Instead, she looked forward to spending Saturday relaxing and watching cable, a guilty pleasure. The following day, she would drive to Chicago.

After unpacking, she donned black running shorts, tank top, and new Adidas. She alternately walked and ran along the river, and explored La Crosse, admiring the lovely university town with its blend of old red brick buildings and scaled-down modern fixtures. The bluffs and the three converging rivers were an oasis after the stress of the last few months.

I've done it this time, gone way overboard. But, hell, it's just a geneal-

ogy. Hundreds of people do genealogies and don't go crazy. If I had any sense, I'd drive back home, but then, how could I write the article? How could I face Elly? No. I have to go on.

~

LATER, she ate dinner, returned to the hotel, and retired early. It was still another four hours to Chicago, and she wanted to hit the road before 6:00 a.m. So, Zara turned on the TV for noise and began packing for the next day's trip to Chicago, placing her notebook, camera, maps, and Martha's photo in her backpack.

She held a Celine Dion CD and smiled. All of her romances had a musical score, so this was no different, but it wasn't the doleful "My Heart Will Go On" since Zara was still torqued off about the *Titanic* movie. Instead, there was a better theme song for Martha and her. The first time she heard "To Love You More,"[2] she blurted out, "That's Martha's message to me," and purchased the CD.

Every word seemed to be written by Martha to her. And even better than love, the lyrics held a promise. She imagined Martha looking down at her and saying, "I've always been there for you, even though you couldn't see me. All that you've gone through will make sense. Oh, and don't worry so much about what people think. They rarely think, anyway."

I'm holding you to your promise, Aunt Martha.

Zara turned the lights out at 10:00 p.m. but lay in bed, staring at the smoke detector's red glow.

That sound. What is that? A train, or maybe a tornado?

The crackling and static grew louder, permeating the space, and Zara finally recognized it.

Oh, my gosh. This sounds like grandpa's shortwave radio!

Her grandfather, Fritz, came to live with her family when she was a kid and occupied the bedroom next to hers. Although she never got a single radio station, the big black suitcase-like device that perched on her grandfather's dresser mesmerized her. He probably bought it in the late 1930s, and even after it was turned on, it took 15 minutes to warm up. She would raise its antenna as high as possible, and then move the circular dial right and left, searching for music or a human voice. Sometimes, she heard airplane noises and ships' horns, but mostly, it played assorted loud fizzing, whizzing, and popping sounds.

Sitting on the edge of the bed, she remembered the night her grandfather died. She had returned from Detroit the previous year and lived in the bedroom she'd had as a child. She was sleeping when a crackling hiss awakened her. It was so loud that she barely heard her grandfather's moans in the next room. *What was going on? Was he playing with the shortwave? Oh, something's wrong, and I must get up and help him.*

But something pinned her to the bed. She froze in terror and closed her eyes. When she opened them, it was morning. She got out of bed, tiptoed down the hall, and cracked open her grandfather's door slightly. He was sitting in his rocking chair, and she stared at his legs.

"Grandpa?"

She couldn't look at his face but walked over to the shortwave. It hadn't been turned on—and it never worked after that.

HER HEART THROBBED while sweat beads trickled down her forehead and into her eyes, and now the incessant crackling and whiff of flowers—also of unknown origin—made her nauseous.

How do I describe an unseen something that's taking over the room? What is this?

She wanted to bolt, but couldn't move.

Dead is dead, but it is definitely not done in this case.

The night progressed, and Zara closed her eyes and inhaled slowly, becoming one with the essence. There was no out-of-the-body awareness. She was joining someone—a lot of "someones," in fact. Several shadowed outlines appeared. Was this her tribe announcing themselves?

As she struggled to focus, the shadows vanished. The veil between death and life splintered that night.

"God," she said while weeping.

I can't hear my heart anymore. Am I dead?

The molecules in the room crumbled and congealed into a smoky haze, and Zara could no longer distinguish shapes. She'd never taken illegal drugs, but this seemed like Elly's description of the LSD trip she'd unwittingly taken in college.

The objects in the room softened, like the inky blacks in a Rembrandt painting.

How can the dark be so warm, so velvet, so comforting? As the essence enveloped her, she calmed down. By 4:00 a.m., exhaustion eclipsed her, and she plunged into an intense slumber.

She woke up at 6:00 a.m. No alarm needed. Scanning the room, she saw nothing in the first embers of morning to hint at the previous night in the netherworld. No time to think. She needed to hit the road.

Journey to Bethania

When Carl Jung developed the theory of collective unconsciousness, he recounted disparate events that defied logic, and yet seemed to direct his path. Although he wasn't sure about these events' meanings, he went out on a limb and said, "Take the hint". Eventually, Jung decided that, "I don't need to believe, I know."

— *Zara's Journal*

She was on the road by 6:20.

Did Pearl create a gateway into another realm—all under the guise of writing a benign family history? Did she know what she was doing? This was like the Book of Thoth in the old *Mummy* movie, filled with riddles, secrets—and death. Zara innocently unlocked the door and was now occupying the world of the manuscript.

No wonder her daily life seemed so ghostly.

Oh, Dad, what do I do? She heard his voice as if he were sitting in the passenger seat.

"It's in the blood."

What is the "it," Dad? What's in the blood?

She suddenly noticed the Beloit, Wisconsin road signs. The Illinois state border was close, and she wasn't sure how she got there.

She crossed into Illinois and pulled into the Elgin McDonald's to review directions and get more coffee.

While walking across the skyway structure above the freeway to the restaurant, she gently tapped her face. It felt good to walk, rotate her shoulders, and stretch her legs. Then, peering out the window at the cars zooming below, she shook her head. *Funny place for a skyway, just over the freeway.*

With its dried grass and parched trees, this part of Illinois was uninspiring, especially after the lush, idyllic Wisconsin countryside. The noonday sun was beating down hard.

While scarfing down coffee and poring over her map, Zara panicked. *Where in the hell is the turnoff to get to Bethania?*

Elly said something about going south on 294. I'll do that.

She noted Justice's location on the wall map in the restaurant, and drew it on a piece of paper to reinforce it. Then she panicked some more.

This is a holiday weekend! Will the cemetery even be open? Oh, man!

She had been walking on water, but now she was sinking. Her eyes were on fire—they were probably dehydrated from the sleeplessness and excessive caffeine intake.

What a dumbass! What was I thinking???

She feared her contact lenses would pop out and didn't have glasses with her. Maybe she wasn't being led after all and was just coasting on a self-concocted fantasy. Perhaps this was part of the trauma that followed the grief of losing her dad.

No matter how hot, teary, thirsty, crazy, and sleep-deprived, she'd finish. Composing herself, she jumped in the car and sped off.

She made several sets of turns and finally saw the sign. *How absurd that Martha's buried in a place called Justice. There's nothing just about any of this.*

Highway 294 and La Grange Road spilled onto South Archer Avenue, and, just as Elly said, there was Resurrection Cemetery. Bethania Cemetery was next to it, and its gates were open!

Her concerns about finding a dilapidated burial ground were unwarranted. Less than ten miles from Chicago, Bethania was in a quiet, pastoral setting near the Forest Preserve. The graveyard's elegant statuary, mausoleums, trees, flowers, and tended grounds were like Grandview Cemetery in Johnstown, PA. Grandview, the final resting place of Zara's grandmother and Martha's sister.

You're both sleeping in beautiful places, dearest ones.

Parking at the entrance, Zara exited the RAV4 and began walking. Her eyes widened when she took in Bethania's expansiveness—a massive, continuous sea of graves.

Damn, it's huge!

Marching to the cemetery's office, she faced a padlocked door. Noticing a groundskeeper watering the grass, she raced over to him, explaining who she was looking for. He expressed regret, saying the office was closed until Tuesday and he couldn't help. "It's too big," he declared. "You'll never find 'em!"

Zara replied, "They're my family. I'll find them. Or they'll find me!" and she stomped off into the center where the oldest headstones were. She saw a small clearing, took a minute to check the writing on a marble headstone, and headed into the thicket. No luck.

Trekking down the rows, scouring names, Zara felt like a human crop duster, snaking up and down, and back and forth again, for 45 minutes. Finally growing overheated, Zara stumbled over a headstone. Although she didn't fall, it felt as if someone had gently pushed her. She headed in the direction in which she had been pointed.

Then she saw it—*Pfeiffer*—on a massive monument. She had parked in front of it—how did she miss it?

Kneeling in front of the dark marble headstone, she pressed her palms together in prayer formation. The great-grandparents' names

— Herman and Bertha Pfeiffer—were inscribed on one side, while her Great-Aunts Frieda and Martha were inscribed on the other. The epitaph above Martha's name read *Auf Die Eastland*. Someone wanted the world to know how she died.

"Hi, family," she said, sobbing, "It's me! Sorry I waited so long...I didn't know... didn't know you were so near."

Sitting on the ledge on Martha's side of the tombstone, she rested her arm and leaned her head against it. She was home!

Just then, a bolt of light flashed across her eyes—kind of like a strobe. The graveyard morphed into a turn-of-the-twentieth century drawing room with chairs, couches, and people. So many people, and so many redheads! They waved to Zara and opened their mouths, but she heard nothing. She smelled the musty wood and clothes, but they faded.

Oh, my god. What just happened? I have to write this while it's happening or I'll forget. I can't forget. Not this time.

She whipped out a notebook and pen from her backpack and began scribbling as fast as she could.

Finding Martha

Plead for me, and tell me why I have chosen thee.
— Emily Bronte[3]

I paused on the ground of a strange place.

This setting of autumn grass, fading flowers, marble, and limestone.

I'd never seen it until this moment and yet found it as if it was my second home.

Yes, I, who was born with zero sense of direction, landed on the precise spot amidst the sea of endless stones.

So, here I am, standing in the early September sun, wondering how I got here.

Why, of all people, did you select someone so disconnected from her nuclear family? Forgive me for questioning you, at once my elder and my younger, but I want to make sure that there wasn't another one you had in mind to carry this out. Whatever this is, I mean, it's not as if you're supplying tremendous clues either.

I pace the ground waiting for you to walk by, to astonish me with the answer, and it would be so easy, and then I could be done with all this, this vexation. You'll throw your arms around me and hug me, and then you will tell me everything. Explain the joke and tell the story the way you wanted it to be told.

THERE IS NOTHING, *not even a merciful breeze to cool me after driving six hours. I don't remember crossing the border from Wisconsin to Illinois, much less how I got here, when I'm sure that I would rather be at the Minnesota State Fair.*

No. I'm just kidding. Just making a joke. That's what I do when I'm scared.

TELL ME. *Why did you wait so long to reveal yourself? Life would have been much easier had I grown up knowing that you existed. Explain, too, why I feel I'm racing against time when time ran out for us long ago.*

You could have found someone of your generation, someone in the next generation. Instead, you chose me and gave me precious little to go by.

How am I to find my way back to you with nothing but photos, a newspaper clipping, and your untimely, tragic demise?

Explain last night, too, that pulsating sound in my room. What was that? I was sure I felt warm fingertips on the back of my hand. Was that you? In the morning light, I told myself it was all in my head, but you know, and I know, that is not true.

You—a forever resident in the land of so long ago—what can I possibly do for you? You want me to save you, is that it? Then will you let me be? Oh, let me be, give me back my life—the life I had before you called me, and set me on this course that leads to a river that won't talk and to a disaster that no one remembers.

They remember and glamorize the Titanic? Why not remember you and everyone else on that terrible day? All 844 of you all! Christ, it was only three years after the Titanic. Would Celine Dion sing about a ship holding young factory workers with unpronounceable last names—immigrants, children of immigrants? People wanting a break, a cruise on Lake Michigan, a picnic at the Indiana Dunes. Just for a day. Was that so much to ask? The damn ship only held you for a few moments before it toppled over.

Chicago, hog butcher of the world, you who have developed a selective loss of memory, you owe me one. You took her life that day, and you robbed me of the one who could have made it all make sense. You owe my family one, and I'm here to collect.

And Western Electric, after Chicago, you're next on my list. You sponsored that picnic, you chartered that ship, and you knew there was something wrong with it.

~

Sunday afternoon, *Labor Day Weekend.*

The air has ceased circulating, and I'm on my knees now, for it seems blasphemous to stand above your bones and whatever else is left of you. What is left of you after eighty-five years? There's no one here, so what do you want me to do? Should I dig and dig and dig until I can break into that coffin that holds you? Is that what you want? Well, maybe I should unearth your tomb just the way you unearthed mine. Now, thanks to all this, I'm starting to look like a lunatic. Do you even care?

Why did you show up now? Just when I was getting back on track after losing my dad?

Why are your life and death suddenly fused into mine? Yeah, I guess I always knew I was holding someone else's life, along with mine, but I'm not *sure I needed the details. It's too powerful, too much of an epic, and I can't contain it.*

I trace the writing on your tombstone with my index finger and am smitten with the swirling ornate German script that says "Auf die East-land," the final words about you.

I halt for a moment, staring at my reflection in your tombstone, your name, your date of birth, your date of death, and how you died, superimposing my darkened, blurred image, branding me from this day forward.

This is who I am.

Tell me now, why did you lead me all the way down here to Bethania to a literal dead end?

What do we do now?

And tell me why the wind refuses to blow?

ZARA HATED LEAVING, but it was time. She already dreaded the ordinary, weighted feelings of being trapped in her own time and in a physical body that could not soar to the heights she needed to scale on this journey.

It no longer mattered that she didn't believe in ghostly visitations, since they now happened without her permission.

I can't fight this anymore, so I might as well roll with it.

Once she drove through Bethania's gates, she would no longer be unconnected.

Great-grandparents Herman and Bertha, I'm alive because you once were. I know you're there, in the ground, but I also know parts of you live on in me. And it's the same with Martha and even baby Frieda. You're here, but you're in me as well.

She faced Martha's, Frieda's, and her great-grandparents' headstone one last time when a soft moth's wing of a voice whispered, "I need you, Zara. I need you."

Zara responded in thought: *You need me? You're dead! What's the point of being dead if you don't know everything? What could you need me for? How could that be? Uh, who am I talking to?*

No explanation. Just the singsong, "I need you, I need you, I need you."

"All right!" Zara said aloud this time, scanning to see if anyone was within hearing distance. "I'll help you, but you better help me, too. Don't leave me this time."

She bowed, said adieu to her family, and walked to her car.

Looking at the headstones in the rearview mirror, she knew she accomplished something by literally driving past her fears. And she also understood that she had altered her life. She didn't feel self-congratulatory but was submerged by guilt over her lifelong stubbornness and apathy concerning her family.

I don't know how to be with you. I mean, Martha, we're not even remotely in the same time zones! How do we bridge the chasm?

THIS JOURNEY CAST light on the odd coincidences throughout her life. The inexplicable connection to Chicago now made sense, and the feelings that consumed her during previous Chicago visits were forceful genetic palpitations. They functioned like a Geiger counter that clicked furiously when it approached radioactive particles!

Who do I tell—besides no one—about this? Would Elly understand?

What's worse? To have never known about you, or to know you so very late in the game? No, it would have been far worse to have gone through life, never knowing you. At least I can bring you back to life and remember you in my corner of the world. Maybe that's all I need to do.

She expected a major epiphany at the gravesite. But no. Instead, more questions bubbled over. Futile or not, she needed to find people who might have known Martha.

Oh God, it's so late in this journey. Could anyone be living who would have known her?

The drive back to La Crosse gave her time to force the experiences of the past 48 hours to jell into something recognizable. That didn't work. She returned to the hotel in La Crosse, sprawled across the bed, and felt more herself when she woke up on Monday at 7:00 a.m.

Happy Labor Day, she said before showering and checking out.

~

SHE WAS RELIEVED to be back in her little apartment on Como Avenue. Opening the door, she smiled at the sunshine streaming through the dusty windows but had no time for contemplation since her story was due in a day. She booted up her computer and rewrote the ending.

How in God's name do I explain what happened?

Reviewing her Polaroids of the gravestones, she tried to absorb it. Why was this so hard?

Remember! Remember! said the not-so-still and not-so-small voice reverberating in her head.

Remember what? I never knew about you, and I never knew your sister, my grandmother. And I didn't even know that my great-grandparents were buried with you.

She thrashed out the story's ending, experiencing the seesaw of euphoria and depression as she explained how it felt to locate her people. Hell, she didn't even know they'd gone missing in the first place.

But their story was stockpiled in her heart and blood, of that she was sure.

While proofreading her article, a loud thud made her bolt from her chair. Zara ran into the kitchen. She saw a box of tissues, paper towels, and bars of soap that she stored atop the refrigerator strewn across the kitchen floor.

Staring at the objects lying on the curling linoleum tiles, she wondered how this happened—since she'd shoved everything to the back of the refrigerator. She replaced the things on top of the fridge, pushing them back further, and returned to her office/bedroom.

BANG-CRASH-BOOM!

Again! Objects were strewn across the floor as if someone sat on the refrigerator and tossed them.

"Come on! These things don't happen. They don't!" she shouted. She placed the items back atop the refrigerator.

She stood, stared, and waited.

Nothing.

She returned to the bedroom, heard the crashing again and darted back into the kitchen. Then, staring at the tissues and paper towels on the floor, she shouted, "Oh, for crying out loud! This has gone on way too long! What do you want? And no more theatrics!"

Silence. Nothing but silence.

I'll call my mother, that's what I'll do, and pretend that none of this had just happened. I'm probably tired, and who knows? Maybe Saint Paul had an earthquake.

"Hi, Mom."

"What's going on?" said Helena. Zara shared a condensed version of her trip.

"Besides Aunt Martha's grave, I found your grandparents' graves, Mom,"

Hearing nothing, she continued talking.

"Did you know they were buried in Chicago?" said Zara.

"No, I didn't," said her mother.

"I brought back some Polaroids. I'll copy them and send them to you—they're really cool. I even took a small rock from near the grave. And I brought back something else, Ma, something I didn't count on."

"What's that?"

"I think," said Zara, staring at the refrigerator, "I brought back Aunt Martha."

Silence.

"Mom, how do you explain...." And Zara talked about the flying objects, expecting her mother, the scientist, to untangle this mess.

"Why did you open that door, Zara?"

"Huh?"

"Zara, you opened the door to peek inside, and now, well, you must go through it," said her mother.

"Ma! What are you talking about? I didn't open anything. And, what the ...? You don't really believe..."

"In much of anything.... or so you thought. I never told you, but when your dad died, things like that started happening. I couldn't reason them away because I saw them. The TV going on by itself, the radio going on and off, lights going on and off."

"Why didn't you tell me?"

"It would have been easy to say I was going delusional. Once. But it kept happening, and I knew, as a scientist, I had to pay attention. Don't draw any conclusions, Zara, but you better pay attention," said her mother.

"To what, Ma?"

"You opened a door, Zara," repeated her mother, "and you have to go through it."

"But Ma...what door? I wasn't looking for anything. I wasn't snooping around for something. This simply happened. I didn't invite it in," said Zara.

"I have to go now," said her mother, who hung up.

Typical!

Zara collapsed into her kitchen chair. Looking up at the ceiling, rivers of tears streamed down her face. Her humble apartment was home for over a decade. No matter what kind of day she had, she could always return to the sanctuary, which was hers alone, until now.

Flying objects aside, there was something more. A presence sharing the space and swirling around her. She saw movement out the side of her eye, only to have it disappear when she looked straight at it. The room on the hot September afternoon chilled. She again felt something like fingertips moving up and down her forearms, and she gasped.

"God," she said, rubbing both elbows. "What do I do now?"

She picked up the phone and called Elly.

"Zara! You got back! You gotta tell me all about it."

"Can I come over? Now!"

"Sure," said Elly. "Everything all right?"

"I'll tell you when I see you. Thanks."

Elly was feeding her cats when Zara pounded on her door.

"Welcome back. I want to hear..."

Zara stormed past Elly and sat at her kitchen table.

"Oh, Elly..."

"Did you have trouble finding it?"

"Oh, I found it. And then some."

7

IS ANYONE OUT THERE?

oly crap, Zara," said Elly, studying Zara. "What happened to you?"

"What?" replied Zara, annoyed at her friend's greeting.

"Look at you! You look as if you lost 10 lbs. in a weekend, and your eyes are sunken and bloodshot. Geez, you didn't go on a bender, did you? What happened in Chicago?"

Zara spit out the details rapid-fire, telling Elly *everything*—from the disembodied noises in the hotel room to discovering the graves, to the falling objects in her kitchen.

Elly sunk into her kitchen chair. "Oh my God, Zara! Anyone else, and I wouldn't believe it. You...well, I believe it. Now what?"

"What do you mean, 'now what?'" said Zara, raising her voice. "It touched me! She touched me," she said, brushing Elly's forearm. "Just like that! She's in my apartment. You gotta come over and see this. You think I have any clue as to what is going on here? Elly, don't you see? I'm cornered!"

"What?" said Elly.

"Geezus, Elly, I don't go looking for the supernatural," said Zara, eyes brimming with tears. "I am not a true believer, or any kind of believer. I didn't think life after death existed. But it does, and now I'm sure of it. You know about these things, so what do I do?"

Elly said, "Zara, it's the middle of the afternoon, but how about some chianti? I think you need it."

"Yeah," said Zara, grabbing the glass of ruby-red liquid from Elly and gulping it.

"Uhh. I think I may need it, too," said Elly, pouring the remainder of the bottle into her glass. "Now, let's say it's true: your Great-Aunt Martha is with you. You conjured her from the grave in Chicago, or she followed you there. Let's say it's true. What's to be afraid of? I mean, she's family, you went to a lot of trouble to find her, she's returned the favor, and you're writing an article about her. So, again, what's to be afraid of?"

Zara sighed. "Lots of things. I grew up with a mother who was a doubting scientist. She had a look. A skeptical look that I didn't take lightly when she cast that look in my direction. Scary! She saw herself as rational, intelligent—her eyes were always on the task at hand, not on accepting fantasy without evidence. Then there was my dad's sister, Magda—the town psychic. It's kind of confusing on my end!"

"Whoa! Slow down, girl. I want to hear more about Magda. Tell me what she was like?"

"She was a character, for sure, but when she would go into a trance, she transformed. Her voice became as clear as glass, and as untouchable as the ice caps of Greenland. And when she was done, she'd let out a deep sigh that I could imagine was the same sigh the Creator made when she brought the universe to life. Unforgettable."

"Back to earth, girl," said Elly, "But you, right now, you're all over the place. No one said you're going to open the next Psychic Friends Network, but something phenomenal happened to you, Zara."

"Wouldn't it freak you?"

"For both my grandmothers, visitations from dead relatives and visions of saints were miracles from God. They expected these things to happen. These were signs that God made to reassure people of his love. Your Aunt Martha made a gesture of love toward you, I think."

"Why me, Elly?"

"Maybe your frequencies match."

"I'm an antenna now, eh?" said Zara. "What if I've gone over the edge finally?"

"Fear not!" said Elly.

"What?"

"That's what the angels say to people when they visit them, and are about to change their lives forever! Fear not, oh, Zara!"

"What do I do, Elly? This trip was supposed to help finish my article and diminish this free-floating anxiety. Now, I'm teetering out of orbit. And those sensations—the feelings of fingers softly caressing my arms at night. Oh, my goodness."

"Most people would find that comforting," said Elly.

"Not when you can't see who's touching you!" said Zara.

Elly instinctively put her arm around her friend, walked her to the couch, and sat with her.

"What do I do now, El?"

"Get the article to your editor, for one thing. Then keep investigating. Maybe Martha wants you to contact the living relatives. I mean, it looks like you have a lot of family right under your nose. Pretty convenient!"

"I'm afraid."

"Get over it then," said Elly, leaning back onto the couch, "Who ya gonna call, *Ghostbusters*? The dearly departed have you over a barrel. There's no one you can talk to outside of me who won't think you're crazy. Face it: you're cornered!"

ZARA TURNED ALL the lights on in her apartment and located the family history. Pearl wrote that Martha's 95-year-old brother, Eddie, was still alive. He lived in Winter, WI, just two hours from the Twin Cities. Zara found his phone number and called him. He said, "Hello." and she introduced herself as the granddaughter of his sister, Annie. He said nothing. She then kept talking about Pearl. He said nothing. Then she mentioned Martha, and he still said nothing.

"Well, umm. Nice talking to you, Uncle Eddie. I'm going to hang up now," she said, downhearted that he wouldn't, or maybe couldn't, talk. She later sent him a note, but didn't think it a good idea to show up on his doorstep.

"Geesh, I hope I didn't scare him to death," she said to Elly.

"I doubt that very much," said Elly. "He might not be able to hear, or maybe he's suffering from some sort of dementia. Why don't you follow Glinda's advice and start at the beginning?"

"What?" said Zara.

"Spend a few days with your Aunt Pearl. She started this whole thing, after all," said Elly. "So, what's the resistance?"

"She's a born-again Christian. Those folks can be so cruel, and I don't want to deal with more family abuse."

"I understand. I do. But look, she's been nice to you so far and demonstrated respect for your writing," said Elly. "Just don't talk about religion. Talk about family history and it will be fine."

"ON THE EASTLAND" was published in early October, and, even with the *Bugle*'s limited distribution area, it found its way to some interesting places.

A writer at the *Star Tribune* called Zara, telling her he'd posted her article on the paper's bulletin board. "Nice piece," he said. "So, when's the book coming out!"

"Book?" said Zara. "No way. I don't do books!"

"Why not? The article is a great basis for a book. Think about it."

Zara had written the article to make sure the *Eastland* Disaster and her Aunt Martha were not forgotten. There was a momentary relief in that, and she hoped that the journey was over now.

But it was just revving up.

8

VISITING PEARL

Zara was both jubilant and panicked about meeting Aunt Pearl again. The thought of spending several days with an older woman she hardly knew, and who was a born-again Christian, upset her stomach slightly. Zara enjoyed older people but was wary of anyone claiming to be "born again," which was often synonymous with hypocrisy and even violence.

The first time someone fired a punch at her—outside of a martial arts class—involved a guy she'd known for years who had become "baptized in the Spirit." The occasion was her coming out to him. He just stood there, and while he was silent, something in his eyes scared her. He wasn't looking at her, but through her. Fortunately, she crouched as he directed his fist toward her skull.

She'd been ducking religious fanatics since.

Pearl probably wouldn't clock her, but she could undoubtedly hurl verbal abuses. Warding off lingering emotional damage from the godly was not one of Zara's strengths. She vanquished these qualms and soldiered on—she had to. She must meet this person who set her life into a tailspin.

On second thought, maybe Pearl already sucker-punched her long-distance.

Taking another long weekend at the end of April would afford Zara time to drive to and from Chicago without stressing out. She even rented a Hi8 Video Camcorder, concluding it would be easier to let the camera run so that she could give Pearl undivided attention. Then she could study the tapes later.

Pearl was older, wiser, and maybe even genuinely spiritual—beyond religious contrivances. And Zara was desperate.

"This is exciting, Zara. Pearl can make sense of all of this—she wrote the story, after all."

"That's what I'm hoping for."

"How much fun it will be for her to have someone interested in her life and her writing!" said Elly, watching Zara squeeze clothes and toiletries inside a beaten-down gym bag.

"God, Zara, don't you have a real suitcase?"

"I have my Amelia Earhart luggage from 1971," said Zara. "It's green with red stripes and stinks—our cat peed in it during one of my visits home from college."

"You still have that luggage?" sighed Elly. "Tell you what, later this summer, let's go through your stuff. Anything you haven't used in 25 years needs to go, and anything with old cat piss tops the list."

"Okay," said Zara, taking a photo from her dresser.

Elly smiled and stood alongside Zara. "That's Pearl? Oh, she's a stunner! Such glamour they had then. Hmm, this looks about 1930, and I love the hat! Doesn't she look like Myrna Loy in *The Thin Man*?"

"My Mom said she looked like Norma Shearer, but she favors Myrna, too. When I was a kid, I fell in love with her photo."

"You have some good-looking women in the family. I mean, look at Martha! She's a doll," said Elly. "And she is the link to Martha—would she have remembered her?"

"No. Pearl was born in February 1916, and Martha died in July 1915," said Zara. "It's funny, but Pearl's the reason my grandmother gave Martha the tickets to the picnic. Grandma was pregnant with Pearl and didn't feel up to an excursion across Lake Michigan."

"Oh, no," said Elly, shaking her head, "This story just got complicated! That's hard to wrap my mind around. Pearl saved her mother's life from inside the womb!"

"Believe me, I've thought of this from every angle," said Zara.

"Well, Pearl. What does she look like now? She's what—82 or 83?"

"Haven't seen her since I was a little kid. My mom said that she's very short and has gained weight. And there's that born-again thing. When I call her, she answers the phone, 'Praise the Lord.'"

"She knows you're gay, right?"

"Not by me telling her, but I'm sure she knows. I hope that blood is thicker than homophobia."

"What will you do if she brings it up?" said Elly.

"Pray," said Zara.

ON THURSDAY MORNING, the last weekend in April, Zara landed at Midway at 8:20 a.m., right on the dot.

"I'll have to stop with the Northwest jokes since they're doing well with being on time."

Fortunately, the rental car place was only a few blocks away, on Cicero. Once she had the car, Zara took a detour before going to Pearl's house, just a few blocks away. She wanted to drive to Bethania Cemetery to visit Martha's grave again.

Zara turned off Archer Avenue, drove through the Bethania Cemetery's gates and immediately saw the Pfeiffer headstone. Parking the car a few feet away, she walked over and knelt in front of Martha's grave.

"Hello again, family," she said aloud, no longer self-conscious about talking to graves. She'd spent enough time in cemeteries, and had seen many people engaged in similar one-sided conversations.

Resting her back against the nearby tree, she removed a photo of Martha from her backpack and propped it against Martha's headstone.

"Aunt Martha, I'm nervous about seeing Pearl, so I wanted to be here with you for a bit to calm down."

She brushed the dust and sand away from Martha's headstone.

"I did the article. I suppose you know that, but, geez, Aunt Martha, please give me a sign that I'm not just talking to myself here! This time, I'll take anything big and dramatic, like the sun falling from the sky. Well, okay, back to the article—people liked it. I hope you liked it, too, because it made me feel better, knowing I'd done something for you. But speaking of Pearl, how do I bring this stuff up with her? How do I explain what you've been doing to my life when I don't understand it? I don't want to scare her."

Remembering Magda, Zara exhaled, closed her eyes, leaned against the tree, and waited for something.

"Sorry, Magda. Maybe I don't have the touch."

She felt empty, then a rush of thoughts streamed in:

Would I see Martha in Aunt Pearl? What of her time and her life would I learn from Pearl? What of her could I see in my life? And Pearl. The Pearl of great price holds the secret treasure. So maybe Martha is not as far away as I think.

Once in the car, Zara stared at the directions and the little map Pearl had drawn.

"*Meticulous directions—reminds me of Mom's preciseness,*" said Zara, who often found exactness too confining.

Zara reminded herself that this beautiful woman, the glamorous reporter whose photo she'd admired since childhood, would be there, hiding in an older person's costume. Inside of Pearl was that young woman, the brash reporter with a burning thirst for knowledge and the truth. Had they been the same age and of the same generation, Pearl and she would have been writing comrades!

PEARL HAD LIVED IN HOMETOWN, Illinois—just nine miles from Chicago—for most of her married life. Hometown was famous for its many duplexes developed for returning World War II GIs and their families.

She pulled into the narrow driveway of the compact side-by-side duplex. The overgrown lawn needed mowing, and the mangled cyclone fence needed replacing.

A round, steel-gray-haired woman stood in the door, smiling and waving.

Opening the door, Zara said, "Hi, Aunt Pearl!"

Pearl embraced, and held Zara, for the longest time, "Oh honey, you can't imagine what it means that you'd spend your money and come all this way just to see me."

Zara stepped back from Pearl as they studied one another: two perfect strangers connected through blood and a story. Zara admired Pearl's high cheekbones and beautiful brown eyes—the only physical remnants of young Pearl.

"I'm sorry I didn't do this before. I can't thank you enough for writing the family history," Zara said, placing her gym bag on the living room floor.

Such meager quarters, filled with a ratty couch, chairs, and tables, drowning in mismatched knickknacks. How does she move in this cracker box?

There was a small TV perched on a table where a large white cat was snoring.

"It's so good to see you, honey. The last time I saw you, you were a kid!" said Pearl. "You look a lot like a Pfeiffer girl."

"I do?" smiled Zara.

"Not your grandmother so much, but definitely like Ida, your grandmother's youngest sister, and Martha. You remind me of Martha."

Zara said, "Well, you sure remind me of my mom! Except she's about 5'8"!"

"She took after her dad with the height. Our mother was short, and so am I. Let's go to the kitchen," said Pearl, reaching for her tripod cane. "We can talk better there. I made some chili, sandwiches, and coffee. You like coffee, don't you?"

The smells wafting from the kitchen—the chili and burning coffee—made Zara gag slightly, but she forced a smile and surveyed the house.

"Mind if I put my stuff down first?" said Zara.

"The bedroom is just down the hall, on the right, next to the bathroom," said Pearl, walking to the kitchen. "Take your belongings to the bedroom. I'd help you, but I'm no good at lifting things."

"I can manage," said Zara, walking down the hallway. Then, reaching for the bedroom doorknob, her hand brushed against something. She gasped and said, "What in fresh hell...!"

The door was blanketed in red, yellow, pink, blue, and rainbow nylon butterflies tacked in no particular pattern or direction. She touched the rainbow butterfly and envisioned being covered in hundreds of them for a Gay Pride Parade and singing, "We Are Family.[1]"

Annoyed that she'd been startled by translucent nylon attached to pipe cleaners, Zara placed her backpack on a small chest of drawers. She saw the swarm extended to both sides of the door, and to the doorjamb. Both sides of the bathroom door were similarly coated in a festive array of faux insects.

Lifting the video camera from its case, she hit the power button, played with the lens, focused, and began filming. Seems easy, she thought, shooting the room, panning in and out of the space. The wallpaper was a crazy lasagna layered in flowers and stripes—and even the ceiling was wallpapered, giving Zara the feeling that she was standing inside a Christmas present. Between the walls and the butterflies, Zara thought, "This is like a scene from *Mothra*."[2]

Walking into the kitchen, Zara said, "Where'd you get the silk butterflies from?"

"Oh, I ordered a kit and enjoyed it so much that I kept ordering more kits. Once I'd learned to make them, I couldn't stop!" laughed Pearl.

"This is something else!" thought Zara, noting the conflicting and competing smells, jumbled decorations, and general disarray.

∾

PEARL'S MEMORY was a force to be reckoned with. Zara placed the video camera on a stool facing Pearl, who began talking while cooking. While Zara offered to help, Pearl would have none of it.

"You just relax, honey. I'll dish up the chili. You can pour the coffee," said Pearl.

Pearl served Zara a bowl of chili with crackers, and Zara said, "Aren't you going to have some too?"

"No, no. This is for you. You relax, and I'll get the pictures and news clippings."

With that, Pearl stepped into a small room off to the side of the kitchen. Zara marveled at Pearl's dexterity with the cane. Placing two boxes of photos on the kitchen table, Pearl led Zara through a labyrinth of memories of growing up in Chicago in the early 1920s. Pearl's mind was a catalog of people, places, and events.

"I'll try to start at the beginning, but I get off track so easily. Just remember to pull me back. When we were growing up, children were instructed to be seen, not heard. Oh, I was so afraid of talking," laughed Pearl. "But I've made up for that!"

"Well, I was born and grew up in the house on West 23rd Street. I lived there with my mother, Annie Pfeiffer Donovan. Annie, of course, was your grandmother. This was my grandparents' house and was where Martha lived, too. Oh yes, Martha walked out of the door that July morning and never returned."

Pearl's eyes sparkled.

"Where was I? Oh yes, now I remember. I loved my grandmother —your Great-Grandmother Bertha. She was the best woman ever, and the heartaches she had—losing her children and her husband and her sweetheart."

Zara's ears perked up. "Are you saying my great-grandmother had a husband *and* a sweetheart?!"

"Of course!"

Zara choked on the last gulp of coffee.

"Bertha was born in a small village in what is now the Poznan region of Poland. She was born in the 1860s, and those were different times. Back then, the children obeyed—they didn't question their elders the way children do now. To talk back? Well, you wouldn't, and Bertha didn't talk back to her mother. Understand?"

"Yeah."

"Bertha's mother, Marie, would be your great-great-grandmother. Are you following me? Marie ruled the home with an iron hand! Her husband, Franz, your great-great-grandfather, was orphaned as a child, and raised by monks in a monastery. Franz was a tender man who would not stand up to his wife. At any rate, Marie arranged Bertha's marriage to Herman, but Bertha already had another sweetheart called Georg! So, Marie broke it up, Bertha married Herman, and the family eventually moved to America."

I come from a family of badass women!

Pearl continued, "Well, as I mentioned, in my day, children also were seen, not heard, so I listened. You learn a lot by just keeping quiet."

"I'm seeing value in silence," smiled Zara.

"When my mother married your grandfather, she moved to Johnstown, Pennsylvania," said Pearl. "I was just twelve and wanted to go with my mother, but she said that I needed to stay in Chicago to take care of my grandmother. My grandmother, Bertha, was a kind person and was always good to me, which helped somewhat. Her sons, Eddie and Herman, were young men at the time, and still living at home. Herman had married, but his wife had left him."

"Wait. It just registered. Your mom—my grandmother—left you behind?" said Zara. "What about your dad? Did you ever live with him?"

"I can hardly remember him—his name was John Donovan, and he was from County Kirk, Ireland. I idealized him a lot because I hardly ever saw him. My mother—your grandmother—left my father when I was about two years old. He died about two years after."

"Why did she leave? That was unusual for a woman to walk out on a man back then."

"Annie was always a free spirit—I think you'd call her that. She liked to get on the streetcars, and the El, and just go places. I don't know if there was anything bad going on in the marriage. Maybe it was hard for Annie, after Martha died, to remain in Chicago."

"Still, that's incredible."

Pearl continued, "Where were we? Grandpa—your Great-Grandpa Herman Pfeiffer—died in 1913 of the flu, and about 18 months later, Martha was killed in the *Eastland* Disaster. So much sorrow for the family in such a short time. My grandma kept Martha's clothes, and I used to wear Martha's green dress! Can you believe it? I was once 100 pounds! Martha was so tiny. Yes, I remember Martha wearing that green dress and those shoes—she wore those button-hole shoes. She would come and kiss me goodnight in that dress when I was a baby."

"Aunt Pearl," said Zara quietly, enunciating each word. "Aunt Martha died before you were born."

Pearl looked up at the ceiling, smiling. "Oh yes, I guess she did."

"But you remember her?" said Zara.

"As clear as you sitting here before me."

Pearl suddenly looked beatific, and Zara wanted to bolt, but she glanced at her watch: 1:45 a.m. She was drained and wondered if Pearl was cracking up under the stress of her visit. But, other than that slight break from reality, Pearl was vibrant and indefatigable—she wanted to keep going.

"Did that scare you, I mean, having Aunt Martha coming to you after she'd died," said Zara.

"What do you mean?" said Pearl.

Now what??

Pearl just told Zara she'd seen a dead woman—and promptly forgot.

Zara looked at her, waiting for an explanation, but Pearl smiled and peered at the kitchen cabinets.

What is she seeing?

I'm losing it! What's next? The silk butterflies morphing into diminutive Mothras, and carrying the house to Oz?

Keep breathing! She told herself.

Zara stood. "Aunt Pearl," she said. "I gotta step out back for a second. I need fresh air—you know, kitty allergies." She pointed to the white cat walking across the kitchen floor.

Pearl jolted as if she'd been awakened from a deep sleep and refocused on Zara. "Okay, honey. I'll put on more coffee."

Once outside, Zara sucked in the cold, spring Chicago air. Staring at the starless black sky, she noticed shadowy vestiges of downtown Chicago in the distance, and her heartbeat amped up.

All that deja vu stuff—no wonder! Our history is interwoven with Chicago. It's our city. Chicago is alive—a force trying to communicate with me. All right. This time, I'm listening, Chicago.

CHICAGO of old was right in front of her, but still outside of her grasp.

This is the craziest thing in my life so far—and that's saying something.

Glancing in the other direction over the porch, Zara watched Pearl's girdle hanging on the line, flapping in the night breeze, which summarily murdered the mood.

And what was happening to Pearl? One minute, she's sharp, and it's like we're two little kids discovering buried riches, and then, on a dime, everything changed. Pearl's weird smile and vacant eyes reminded me of an old horror film where the sweet old lady turned into an evil entity, murdering her visitor! Perhaps this weird in-and-out-of-reality turnstile was a part of the aging process. Still, Pearl thought she saw Martha. Maybe Pearl needed rest, but even if she didn't, Zara did.

Zara opened the back door.

"Feeling better?" said Pearl.

"Oh yeah. Allergies are a pain, and I have to get out of the house occasionally," she fibbed. "Maybe you're tired, Aunt Pearl. I'm keeping you up way past your bedtime!"

"I've never felt more alive," said Pearl. "Your visit does my heart good! I made some fresh coffee, so let's keep talking."

Zara groaned but didn't want to disappoint. Besides, she knew that this first visit could also be their last, given Pearl's age.

"Aunt Pearl, I want to write a more extensive article about Aunt Martha and the *Eastland,* and I was hoping you could explain something."

Pearl nodded.

"When you sent me your family history, this information was new to me, and I wanted to learn everything."

Pearl studied Zara intently.

"But when I was knee deep in the investigation, things started happening. Bizarre things that I can't explain. Before I went to see Martha's grave, I was alone in my motel room. But I was sure someone else was with me. I felt it. And, I saw something, but when I stared at it, it vanished."

"What else?"

"The next day, when I got to Bethania, I found the family graves, even though I'd never been there. Later, when I was back home, and finishing the article, stuff kept getting knocked off my refrigerator as if someone was throwing it. All these things that defied reality as I knew it," said Zara. "What do I do, Aunt Pearl?"

"Oooh, the blood of Jesus. Ooooooh, the blood of Jesus cover me," said Pearl, closing her eyes.

"Hey—what's wrong?" said Zara.

"I'm praying for God's protection from the dark spirits as I tell you these stories," said Pearl.

"Aunt Pearl, you don't believe... No! Stop it! Aunt Martha is disconcerting, but she's no dark spirit."

"Zara, I'm not talking about Aunt Martha, but when you open yourself up to spirits, you have to be careful what gets in."

"Aunt Pearl, c'mon. You have faith in Jesus, right? So don't you think He's more powerful than the, uh, dark side? So why are you afraid? 'Greater is He that is in you than he that is in the world,'" said Zara, relieved that she remembered that particular Bible verse.

"You're right, honey, you're right. But we will claim the blood of Jesus over all of this," said Pearl, sitting down.

"Okay" said Zara.

"So," said Pearl, staring into Zara's face. "Martha's visiting you, too. Just like she used to visit me."

Zara alternated between relief and shock that Pearl finally remembered the encounter with Aunt Martha.

"I saw her once as a kid but didn't know who she was," said Zara.

"How did you know it was her?" said Pearl.

"The news clipping you sent triggered that memory. And a face like hers, well, it's hard to forget. I haven't seen her since then," said Zara, "but I feel her fingers at night, touching the back of my hand and arm. I sense her sometimes, and I smell flowers that aren't there —lilacs, mostly. Supernatural things? I thought I'd outgrown them, but I can't ignore what's happening. The more I try, the worse it gets!"

"I see."

"Why is she doing this? I think she wants something from me, but what?"

"I was just a kid, too," said Pearl. "And only in the last ten years did I remember."

"Oh, my,"

"By the time I got to this age, I thought I'd be as wise as your great-grandma, but I'm not. And I don't know what she wants."

Zara touched Pearl's hand. "I get why she'd visit you, but why would she bother with someone who never even heard of her? Why set me on this obstacle course?" said Zara.

"Maybe she just wants to say 'hello.' Too bad someone didn't save Martha like that farmer who saved Aunt Julia in the Johnstown Flood," Pearl said.

"What??!" said Zara, nearly tipping over in the chair.

"You rock in that chair just like Uncle Eddie. Uncle Eddie was Martha's brother, you know!"

"Yes, I know, I know. But what's this about the Johnstown Flood?" said Zara.

"You know about the Johnstown Flood of 1889," said Pearl.

"Like I know the back of my hand—I was born there too, but I didn't know we had a relative in the Flood."

"Your great-grandfather's sister and her husband were the first ones to come to America and settled in Johnstown just before the Flood."

"Okay," said Zara, rocking wildly. "Tell me about her."

"Julia Rohr, your great-grandfather's sister, and her husband had a boarding house in downtown Johnstown. When the Flood came, she was swept away by the current while clutching her baby in her apron. A farmer grabbed her by her hair—women had long hair then—and saved her. She and the farmer waited out the Flood on his barn's roof. That's how high the water was."

"Don't you think it is more than a fluke that we've had two relatives in two major water-related catastrophes?"

"You're right. Now you have me thinking about it differently. What could it mean? In the Bible, God tells us you die and rise again in baptism. You went to seminary. What else does water mean?"

"Hmm...well...Jesus calls himself the Living Water. Remember? When he talked to the Samaritan woman."

"Oh yes! Jesus answered her, 'If you knew the gift of God and who it is that asks you for a drink, you would have asked him, and he would have given you living water.[3]'"

"Hey Pearl! That's pretty impressive! Water figures prominently in the scriptures. There's the story where the world is nearly destroyed by water. But the stories are mostly about cleansing, new life, and purification."

"Well, look at it this way. Both Julia and Martha are dead, and I don't know how much longer I'll be around. So, we all must cross over the Jordan River," Pearl began singing the old hymn.

"Water and rivers seem to be an ongoing theme. Two female relatives involved in major water-related tragedies—one in the nineteenth century, and the other in the early twentieth. One is saved. One dies. That's two too-many coincidences for me."

"That's because you're a journalist. You see patterns and you want to get to the truth," said Pearl.

"I'm used to writing stories with neat little conclusions. I make meaning out of painful things—makes them hurt less."

"Life hasn't been easy for you, sweetie."

"I made it this far! But I can't tie up Aunt Martha's story—it is like a ball of yarn that keeps unraveling with no end. Just one tease after the other," said Zara.

She hesitated and locked eyes with her aunt. "Pearl. Really. Why did you give me the family history? Did you know what it would do to me?"

"Well, truth be told, you were my last hope. I sent it to other relatives, and no one even thanked me! So, I prayed, and God put it on my heart. He said you'd be the only one who'd carry the family stories forward. You'd weave it into a tapestry. You're a courageous young woman, Zara, being out on your own all these years. The story needs someone with courage, and God knows that."

Zara teared up and hugged Pearl. "You're too kind, Aunt Pearl. Believe me, I'm not very courageous. Not at all. And it's not false modesty."

"But you lived in inner-city Detroit with that church community. You moved to Minnesota by yourself with no family, at least no family that you knew of."

"That wasn't courage—that was survival. I had to get away from home. And all those years of living in the Twin Cities—with Falling Brook and all those relatives close by—and Uncle Eddie just a few hours up north! Well, I never knew. Now it seems too late."

"You just felt drawn to Minnesota? You didn't know about all the family you had nearby?" said Pearl.

"How could I know? I just moved to Minnesota because, well, it seemed to call out to me. It was the first place that felt like home—except, of course, Johnstown—my heart will always be there. Cleveland never felt like home."

"Praise the Lord. That was God calling out to you through your ancestors."

"The ancestors I never knew I had. That's why I'm stuck on this, Pearl. It would have been one thing to grow up and know my mom's complete family history. But I didn't. Heck, I only met you once. I'd never met the other Chicago relatives, so it didn't connect. But there was always something about Chicago, even though I never felt compelled to live here. Yet I *felt* compelled to relocate to the upper Midwest and had no clue why. And Wisconsin! Do you know how many times I stayed in Eau Claire, which is right next to Falling Brook, for weekend getaways?!"

"Did you really? Ooh, I feel the witness of the Holy Spirit when you say that. That's wonderful and means you could hear their voices," said Pearl. "Your heart heard their voices. You're more like them than you know. You're like your grandmother. She was so independent—to up and leave. You're like Martha with your boy's clothes and Ida with her art talent."

"And I'm like you with your writing talent."

Pearl laughed.

"Well, Aunt Pearl, I have to admit it, I'm hitting the wall, and I've gotta hit the hay for a few hours."

"Sweet dreams. And, Zara, I can't tell you how wonderful it is to have you here! I haven't felt this good in years," said Pearl.

"Are you going to sleep?" said Zara.

"Who me? No, I don't sleep much anymore. I'm going to stay up and watch *The 700 Club*! Do you want to watch it?" said Pearl.

Zara shuddered. "Ummm, not me! I'm going to sleep! Good night, Aunt Pearl," said Zara, leaning over to kiss her aunt's forehead.

Zara laid down on the tiny cot in the sliver of a bedroom. When she closed the bedroom door, and turned out the light, the silk butterflies on the back of the bedroom door cast ominous shadows on the walls.

"Those damn butterflies! What's next? Frogs, boils, water turning to blood? Damn, I'm tired." Closing her eyes, she sunk into a deep sleep.

~

THE FOLLOWING MORNING, Zara opened her eyes and screamed! A small, round figure was standing over her.

"Oh, Aunt Pearl, I forgot where I was," said Zara. "What time is it?"

"About eight o'clock, honey, and I didn't mean to scare you! Let's get ready and go to Bethania, and I can show you Julia Rohr's grave, too," said Pearl. "She is buried in Bethania, too. I haven't been there in years, but I think Julia and her children and Uncle Rohr are buried toward the back of the cemetery."

"Aunt Pearl, did you sleep at all?"

"Not much. I am just so happy that you're here."

"Me, too," said Zara. "Let me take a shower first. You have more coffee, right?"

"Sure do, honey. I just bought some nice instant coffee just for you."

The thought of instant coffee made Zara queasy, but she desperately craved caffeine.

Heading toward Bethania

As they pulled out of the driveway, Pearl shouted in a loud quivery voice, "The Blood of Jesus, the Blood of Jesus," and Zara jolted.

"Hey-ah, Aunt Pearl," said Zara. "Could you let me know when you're going to do that? I'm a little edgy driving around in an unfamiliar city."

"Of course, sweetie, of course," said Pearl. "Just go on Cicero. When we get to West 79th, make a left and take it all the way to Justice. The cemetery's on Archer Avenue. Goodness. I haven't been to Bethania in at least 20 years. Certainly not since your uncle got sick."

"Pearl, do you know why the family ended up in Bethania, I mean, why Justice, Illinois?" said Zara.

"I don't know," said Pearl. "Bethania was a new cemetery back when Martha was killed, and it was probably built because they needed space. Plus, people from Chicago could take the streetcar up Archer Avenue to get here and make a day of it. People used to have picnics at cemeteries, you know."

Parking the car in front of the Pfeiffer grave, Zara leaped out to assist Pearl, who had already opened the door and planted her cane on holy ground.

"Hold it, Pearl," said Zara. "Let me help you!"

"I'm so happy, so happy to be here," said Pearl, charging past Zara to the Pfeiffer headstone.

"It's beautiful, the stone," said Zara.

"Ruhet in Frieden, Martha Pfeiffer, auf die *Eastland*," said Pearl.

"Rest in peace, Martha Pfeiffer. On the *Eastland*," said Zara.

"You know your German, honey. That's good because it will come in handy. That inscription must have cost them a lot of money," said Pearl.

"Auf die *Eastland*?" said Zara.

"Yes. Those words, *Auf die Eastland*—on the *Eastland*-—were extra, beyond the cost of the headstone," said Pearl. "Look on the other side at the inscriptions for your great-grandparents. They only give names and dates. No description of how they died."

"But someone wanted us to know how she died," said Zara. "It's a message from the past."

The women stood silent and faced their ancestors' graves. Then, finally, Zara turned toward Pearl, who had tears streaming down her cheeks, and put her arm around her.

"I'll soon be joining them," said Pearl. "And I'll be overjoyed—I miss them so much. But Zara, go on and tell the story. And also tell your mother that I'm sorry."

"Sorry? What?" said Zara.

"I've carried this all my life," said Pearl. "When we got the word in Chicago that my mother was dying—I deliberately took a later train, hoping she'd be dead by the time I got to Johnstown."

"Why?" said Zara.

"Because I knew she'd ask me to take care of your mother," said Pearl.

"Aunt Pearl, you were only thirteen years old," said Zara. "Even if Grandma would have asked you to take care of my mother, that wouldn't have been possible."

"But I feel guilty," said Pearl.

"Aunt Pearl, come on," said Zara. "I don't think God expected you to act like an adult in that situation. You were a kid, and you ended up an orphan. There's nothing that you could have done for a baby."

"I still feel bad," said Pearl, weeping.

"I know you feel bad, but please remember that my mom was fine. She stayed in Johnstown, and she had her dad, her uncle and aunt, and lots of cousins. She lived in a twenty-two-room mansion! That's better than you or I ever did, eh?"

"I guess, I guess," said Pearl.

"Had you taken Mom back to Chicago, how could you have cared for her? After all, your grandmother was old at that point, and then she died just a couple of years after my grandmother died. So, then what would you have done?" said Zara.

"You're right," said Pearl.

"It all worked out. Mom had her father's family, and she made it to adulthood intact. She was brought up in wealth, attended college, and got to do things that women of that generation rarely did. You did nothing wrong."

"Thank you, Zara," said Pearl, dabbing her eyes. "Tell me, do you believe?"

"Believe?" said Zara.

"Yes, are you saved?" said Pearl. "You know your scriptures."

"Yep. In Greek, Hebrew, and Aramaic!"

"Well?"

"Uh.... I think Jesus and his message, and his actions were wonderful," said Zara. "But religion has sullied and destroyed most of that. It's perverted his message in such a way that it's not even recognizable. How they can turn love into hate is beyond me."

Pearl was silent and then said, "I don't believe in religion either. I believe in a relationship with God through Jesus."

"That's good," said Zara. "Relationships are stronger than religions."

Still, Pearl seemed unconvinced, which perplexed Zara to no end.

She's such an intelligent woman, so why is her religion based on fear of a punishing God, the devil, and imaginary demons and monsters. Oh, Pearl, why are you giving your extra money to Pat Robertson, that electronic Elmer Gantry. Faced with a demon or Pat Robertson, I'll take the demon— far less vicious.

Meeting Cousin Ruthie

On the way back from Bethania, Pearl said, "Let's go visit Cousin Ruthie, since she lives close, just off Pulaski. I haven't seen her since...you know."

"Since you asked her to leave," said Zara. "Mom told me."

Pearl shook her head. "Poor Ruthie, I can't get around like I used to, and Ruthie is close to 90 and in that chair. She kept forgetting things, kept going to the bathroom in her chair, and I couldn't..."

"Of course not, Pearl. I mean, it was noble of you to try," said Zara. "Tell me who Ruthie is again since it's hard, keeping these relatives straight."

"Ruthie is your grandmother's oldest sister—Emma's—daughter —your cousin, once removed," said Pearl.

"Okay," said Zara, repeating "Grandmother's oldest sister's daughter," to herself.

Pearl directed Zara down a street. They parked and walked to Ruthie's house.

"She's living with her son, and her mind is good—not her health. Been in the wheelchair for years," said Pearl. "She was the last one to live in the family house, but they forced her to leave. That's how she ended up with me for a while. She only left there two years ago, and I guess it was filled with garbage, cat poop, and pee."

"Eeek," said Zara. "But she was in the family house, where Martha lived. She's old enough to have remembered Martha."

Zara and Pearl inched down the stairs of the old Chicago brownstone, not too far from the Indian statue, the one with the arrows in his head, and Gertie's Ice Cream parlor of *Wayne's World* fame. Zara had even had ice cream there once a long time ago, without knowing that family members were just a stone's throw away.

"We can ask her about Martha," said Pearl, knocking on the door.

~

A BALDING, middle-aged man answered the door, his drooping mustache the only thing lower than his frown. "Yeah, c'mon in," he said.

"Hi Jimmy, this is your cousin, Zara. This is Ruthie's son," said Pearl.

"Hey," said Zara.

Jimmy stared at her, grunted, and walked away just as Ruthie emerged from a side room, swinging her wheelchair deftly around the corner. She glared at Pearl. "What kept ya so long? Well, don't stand there! Just sit down."

Zara and Pearl dropped to the couch as the older woman wheeled closer, her eyes locking onto Zara, who feared that she might run her down.

"Ruthie," said Pearl, "This is..."

"I know who this is, for godssake," shouted Ruthie, blue eyes looking like the flame of a pilot light.

"Here!" said Ruthie, throwing a photo at Zara. "Do you know who this is?"

Zara studied the old photo of a woman in an enormous hat and parasol.

Ruthie answered for her, "That's your grandmother. You can have that photo, too."

"Thank you," said Zara.

"Where'd that sonofabitch go now?" shouted Ruthie.

"I'm goin' upstairs, Ma!!" shouted Jimmy.

"No good sonofabitch," said Ruthie, "Stinking alcoholic, just like his father."

Pearl changed the subject, "So, how are you feeling, Ruthie?"

"How do you think I'm feeling, Pearl?! I'm in this goddamn wheelchair. I feel like hell!" said Ruthie.

"And you," she pointed at Zara, whose eyes widened. "I met your mother once, and did she ever say anything about me?"

"She mentioned it," Zara lied.

"WELL, that's something since she was a baby. Too damn bad, y'know. The family got blown to pieces when everything happened. You don't recover from some things. I don't care how many damn years go by," said Ruthie.

Zara, having gotten over the shock of meeting Ruthie, began studying her. She appeared healthy, with bright blue eyes, nearly wrinkle-free skin, and a shock of thick white hair like a Cossack hat perched on her head. She could almost leap out of that wheelchair and start boxing with someone, Zara thought.

"Ruthie, what do you mean?" said Zara, fearing for her life. "What was blown to pieces?"

Ruthie looked down at her hands, which began shaking. "Martha died, and the whole thing went up in smoke. I was there, you know. Did you know that? It was a warm day, and Martha was in that coffin with the pink dress and the garland of flowers in her hair. I was four years old when it happened. I remember it. I remember it better than I remember yesterday."

"You lived in the house," said Zara.

"Everyone died or moved, and I didn't want the house to go to strangers. My no-good sonofabitch husband was dead by then. Boys were gone. But her dress and her shoes—they'd move around. It made me crazy, so I had to burn them."

"What dress and shoes?" asked Pearl.

"Martha's!" said Ruthie.

Zara gasped. "You burned her dress and shoes?? Why?"

"You try living with that, Missy. Things moving when there's no one there! I burned 'em, yeah, I burned 'em!"

Zara leaned back into the couch and stared at Pearl, who forced a smile.

"How's Patsy," said Pearl, referring to the small dog lying near Ruthie.

"She gets around better than I do," said Ruthie.

"And you," said Ruthie, pointing a bony, gnarled finger at Zara. "You have awakened the dead, haven't you? Well, good luck living with that!"

Zara stared at Ruthie and said, "How do you know?"

"You think just because I'm old that I don't see? I see who you are and what you've done."

"Well," said Pearl, "We have to go now. Zara has to catch a plane later today." Zara was startled. Her plane didn't take off until the following morning.

"Okay, Okay," said Ruthie, moving forward. She extended her hand to Zara.

Zara took her hand and said, "Goodbye, Cousin Ruthie."

"Listen, kid, I wish you all the luck in the world. Unfortunately, you're going to need it."

"Thanks," said Zara.

As they left, they were silent, but once in the car, Zara turned to Pearl.

"What was that all about?" said Zara. "Was Ruthie always like that?"

"More or less. She just became more that way as she aged. We all do," said Pearl.

"She burned Martha's dress and shoes! I wanted to throttle her," said Zara.

"She was always so afraid of them, claiming they moved around and such," said Pearl. "Well, honey, that's that. Would you like to go to Denny's on Cicero? I saved up all these coupons when I knew you were coming."

A Grand Slam® breakfast was the last thing on her mind at the moment, but Zara said, "Sure. Just tell me how to get there."

As much as Zara detested chains, she was deliriously happy to sit at Denny's with Pearl. Denny's—the only predictable thing on this trip so far.

Pearl and Zara reviewed more photos that evening, including one of Pearl and Ruthie taken when the two were decades younger.

"That's Ruthie and you!?" laughed Zara. "Goodness! You both were just gorgeous! Did you know how pretty you were?"

"Honestly, I never thought that way," said Pearl. "Back then, women were taught not to think much of themselves. You never wanted people to think you were conceited, but I sometimes wish I had been born in your generation. I would have done some things differently."

"Like what?" said Zara.

"Well, I would have liked to live with my lady friend, Aggie. She and I worked for the paper. You couldn't do that back then, live with a lady friend, because people would think you were bad," said Pearl. "Look at what you've been able to do, all by yourself. Tell me, did you ever live with any of your lady friends?"

"No, I never lived with any of my lady friends," said Zara. "I really like living by myself, I guess."

"Me, too," said Pearl. "It may sound strange, but I've never been happier since I've been living alone."

"Doesn't sound strange at all," said Zara.

Zara refrained from probing deeper, but Pearl's comments about her "lady friend" sent her heart soaring. Still, she didn't want to offend her, but she wondered if she, Pearl, and Martha might share something besides DNA? Maybe she'd never know.

WHILE RUMMAGING THROUGH PHOTOS, Zara saw hordes of relatives that she never heard of.

"I am so overwhelmed, but in the best possible way," said Zara.

"I am so pleased that a young person like you is interested in our family," said Pearl.

Then the topic returned to the *Eastland.*

"Aunt Pearl, why was the *Eastland* Disaster erased from history? Why didn't I hear about it growing up?"

"Hmm, I just recalled something," said Pearl, reaching for her cane and lifting herself from the chair. Zara cringed, watching the enormous struggle it took Pearl to move from one room to the other and followed Pearl back to the sewing room.

"Honey," said Pearl. "Could you reach the upper shelf in the closet and bring me those folders?"

Zara obeyed and grabbed two overstuffed folders as the dust flew.

Zara sneezed and handed the folders to Pearl, saying, "Aunt Pearl, I have to get a tissue from my purse."

She sneezed several more times before reaching her purse. Then, blowing her nose, she stared out the back window, glancing at vestiges of the city obscured by smog and buildings.

If only I could see the real Chicago, the Chicago of Martha's time. Right now, 1999 is getting in my way.

"Zara, honey, I have something," called Pearl from the sewing room.

Walking into the room, she saw Pearl seated at her desk, holding several sheets of yellowed papers. She handed the first one to Zara, who read silently.

LOOKING 'EM OVER

By CARL SANDBURG

In the second-largest city in America, a passenger steamship, tied to the dock, loaded with 2,500 working people dressed in their picnic clothes, topples slowly and sinks to the river bottom like a dead jungle monster shot through the heart. Over 1,000 men, women and children, trapped like rats in a cellar, are drowned....

...Behind the thousand working class dead of the Eastland is the story of why they started on a picnic the day of their deaths. They went because they were afraid of their jobs. Of course, they didn't know they were going to die on the Eastland. The Western Electric Company for which they worked didn't know they were off on a death harvest instead of a lake and woods outing. But what the Western Electric workers know and what the officers of the Western Electric know is this terrible fact:

There was no choice for the wage slaves of that corporation. The foremen came to the employes [sic] with tickets. The employees bought tickets and went to the picnic because it was part of their jobs...

...Did the Western Electric offer the workers white hats and white shoes free for this parade? It did not. It told the workers they would be expected to have white shoes and so each paid from a dollar to two dollars out of their slim pay envelopes. And the white hats were outrightly forced on each one at a price of thirty cents apiece.

Grim industrial feudalism stands with dripping and red hands behind the whole Eastland affair.[4]

∾

ZARA SHOOK her head and returned the paper to Pearl. "Carl Sandburg wrote about this? I only knew him as a poet. Lordy! Western Electric forced the employees to get on this thing? And Martha should have never been there in the first place!"

Pearl also shook her head, nearly in unison with Zara, "I know, sweetheart. Back then, working-class people had few choices. People today don't realize how bad it was."

Zara paced. "I'm so angry right now. Just because we were immigrants or children of immigrants, we were treated as if we were..."

"Dispensable," finished Pearl. "There's one more piece you need to read from Sandburg. It's a poem."

Zara took the document from Pearl and read aloud.

∾

EASTLAND
By Carl Sandburg

The *Eastland*
Let's be honest now

For a couple of minutes

Even though we're in Chicago.

Since you ask me about it,

I let you have it straight;

My guts ain't ticklish about the *Eastland*.

It was a hell of a job, of course

To dump 2,500 people in their clean picnic clothes

All ready for a whole lot of real fun

Down into the dirty Chicago River without any warning.

Women and kids, wet hair and scared faces,

The coroner hauling truckloads of the dripping dead

To the Second Regiment armory where doctors waited

With useless pulmotors and the eight hundred motionless stiff

Lay ready for their relatives to pick them out on the floor

And take them home and call up the undertaker...

Well I was saying

My guts ain't ticklish about it.

I got imagination: I see a pile of three thousand dead people

Killed by the con, tuberculosis, too much work and not enough fresh air and green groceries

A lot of cheap roughnecks and the women and children of wops,

and hardly any bankers and corporation lawyers or their kids, die from the con-three thousand a year in Chicago and a hundred and fifty thousand a year in the United States-all from the con and not enough fresh air and green groceries...

If you want to see excitement, more noise and crying than you ever heard in one of these big disasters the newsboys clean up on,

Go and stack in a high pile all the babies that die in Christian Philadelphia, New York, Boston, and Chicago in one year before aforesaid babies haven't had enough good milk;

On top of that pile put all the little early babies pulled from mothers willing to be torn with abortions rather than bring more children into the world--

Jesus, that would make a front page picture for the Sunday papers

And you could write under it:

Morning glories

Born from the soil of love,

Yet now perished.

Have you ever stood and watched the kids going to work of a morning?

White faces, skinny legs and arms, slouching along

rubbing the sleep out of their eyes on the go to hold their jobs?

Can you imagine a procession of all the whores of a big town, marching and marching with painted faces and mocking struts, all the women who sleep in faded hotels and furnished rooms with any man coming along with a dollar or five dollars?

Or all the structural iron workers, railroad men and factory hands in mass formation with stubs of arms and stumps of legs, bodies broken and hacked while bosses yelled, "Speed-no slack-go to it!"?

Or two by two all the girls and women who go to the hind doors of restaurants and through the alleys and on the market street digging into the garbage barrels to get scraps of stuff to eat?

By the living Christ, these would make disaster pictures to paste on the front pages of the newspapers.

Yes, the *Eastland* was a dirty bloody job--bah!

I see a dozen *Eastlands*

Every morning on my way to work

And a dozen more going home at night.[5]

*** Con = Consumption

"OMIGOD!" said Zara. "Carl Sandburg wrote all of this about the *Eastland*?! He was my favorite poet in high school, and I remember him as a white-haired grandpa character. But he was an investigative reporter!"

"Yes, he was," said Pearl.

"Well, Sandburg has at least a partial answer why the *Eastland* was ignored."

"What do you mean?" said Pearl.

"Western Electric! Sandburg was hinting at a corporate cover-up! Geez, nothing ever changes, does it? I mean, he could be writing about today because that's what they do."

"You think that could be it?" said Pearl.

"Like Mae West said, 'the story's so old, it should have been set to music long ago.' I can't think of anything else! Sure, they run a story for a brief time and then silence the journalists. And damn Western Electric—they forced those employees to go to that picnic for a photo-op, forced them to buy the white shoes and hats. Scoundrels. Why didn't the people rebel?"

"What kind of power would the people have had? There were no unions, no workers' rights. If the remaining Western Electric workers had rebelled, then they would have risked losing their jobs, and then where would they be? There was no unemployment insurance, social security, welfare, nothing like that."

"They were like prisoners then. The message to them was 'keep quiet or else,'" said Zara.

"Exactly," said Pearl.

"Similar to the Johnstown Flood. I mean that wasn't a simple act of nature since it resulted from the negligence of the Pittsburgh elite who owned this little resort—the South Fork Hunting and Fishing Club. They ignored warnings about the South Fork Dam's structural problems, and then, on May 31, 1889, it just kept raining. Carnegie and the rest bailed, and I don't know if they were ever held responsible."

"You're right," said Pearl. "I never saw the connection until now. You're smart, Zara."

"Well, I come from a long line of brilliant women! I wonder if that's one of the many reasons that Martha is refusing to leave," said Zara.

"You can't change the past, honey," said Pearl.

"Perhaps—but I know you can change the future," said Zara.

IT WAS 5:00 A.M., and although she didn't have to go to the airport that early, she was agitated and needed to walk and disperse all the built-up energy.

The previous night, Pearl said, "Wake me up before you leave, honey."

Zara tiptoed into the tiny closet of a bedroom where the older woman was sleeping—peacefully exhausted from spending two days in the past.

"Aunt Pearl," whispered Zara, "I'm leaving now."

Pearl opened her eyes and smiled. Zara knelt, and they embraced. "Thank you so much, Aunt Pearl. It's so cool getting to know you. You've given me a lot."

"May the blood of Jesus cover you," said Pearl.

May our ancestors guide you and welcome you home. Zara felt that this would be the last time she'd see Pearl on this side of eternity.

She kissed Pearl on the forehead and whispered, "Thank you for everything."

The two women—one in the middle and one at the end of the age spectrum—looked at each other, smiling.

DRIVING PAST BETHANIA, the gates were shut, and fog blanketed the grounds, making them look like the otherworldly landscape that they were. Zara stopped and stared at the Pfeiffer grave through the bars and cried, weeping from joy. And sorrow.

9

TRACING HER STEPS

Dancing with your memory, your essence, was the smoothest choreography. Sometimes you lead, sometimes, I take over, putting my spin on things, imprinting our journey together with my style, so it is as much mine as yours. And it is truly and surely becoming ours.
—*Zara's journal.*

Zara sprinted to Elly's place.

While giving the blow-by-blow account of the three days with Pearl, Elly shook her head.

"Whoa, girl! Your Aunt Pearl, Cousin Ruthie, and now you! Three women in your family, independent of each other, claimed to have seen or felt Martha!"

"Yeah," said Zara. "I wasn't the first, and since Pearl and Ruthie saw her, I'm almost inclined to believe that I'm not making this up."

"Of course not!" said Elly. "I'd believe you regardless, but that's three people, one of whom was so scared that she burned Martha's dress and shoes!"

"Please," said Zara, waving her hand. "I can't stand thinking about that!"

"Hmm. This is significant—really, really momentous."

"I get that, Elly. I do, but what in the blazes does it mean? And why does Martha choose certain ones of us to haunt?"

"Dunno. But one thing's certain—the *Eastland* Disaster has been blotted out from the telling of Chicago's history, and that makes no sense. Someone or something—such as a corporation—didn't want to draw attention to its own complicity. Carl Sandburg's *Eastland* article and poem corroborate that. I always loved Sandburg, and he could hold a corporation's collective feet to the fire."

"You think Martha wants to bring this crime to our attention and to get justice?" said Zara.

"When that many are obliterated in a single event, that creates a deep wound. Can you imagine the horror of witnessing that? Talk about post-traumatic stress! And the survivors? I'm sure their lives were never the same," said Elly.

"Finally, there are families like mine who lost loved ones. How did they go on?" said Zara.

"C'mon. Let's take a walk. I need some fresh air," said Elly.

"Sure."

"Mind if we stroll around your alma mater?"

"Hey, it's just across the street, so why not? I've made peace with it. Mostly."

The women left Elly's house and walked toward the campus of Martin Luther Seminary, with Zara leading.

"Hey, slow down! It's not like you're late for class!"

"Old habits die hard!"

"Say what you will. This place has a fantastic bookstore," said Elly.

"Agree. See that other building, the monstrosity with the ginormous cross planted in the front? That's my old dorm!"

"Geez! It looks as if they should have condemned this years ago. Reminds me of the scene in *The Trouble with Angels* [1] where Hayley Mills' character first sees Saint Francis Academy, gasps in horror, and says, 'It's positively medieval!' What—umm—style is that?"

"Early Lutheran Pietist, otherwise known as No-Style-At-All!" said Zara

"You're full of it," said Elly.

"Uh-uh! Don't forget. I have a master's degree from this erstwhile institution and deep knowledge of *formgeschichte, heilsgeschichte,* and *BULLgeschichte!*"

Elly stopped walking and took Zara's arm. "Every so often, it washes over me—what you've gone through. They hurt you, didn't they? You've paid such a price for simply trying to exist."

Zara stared straight ahead and clenched her jaw.

"You should have met the little zealot that once was me. I had it all figured out by the time I was 18 and was prepared to serve the church for the rest of my life. So how did I know that the love they proclaimed to have for everyone didn't apply to me?"

Elly grabbed Zara and pulled her close, "If I could, I'd change the world for you so that you'd be safe."

"Ah, thanks, El. Now, don't you cry. I'm used to it, and I've survived, and occasionally thrived. But, unfortunately, many of my cohorts didn't."

"And now, you've been given a precious jewel."

"The best," said Zara.

"So, your grandmother identified Martha at the morgue?"

"According to Pearl."

"Lord, God! No wonder your grandma wanted to escape Chicago. Then she dies when your poor mom was just three years old."

"It's a curse," said Zara.

"I never believed in curses until now."

They continued hiking up the hill, through the trees, and toward another set of buildings.

"Hey, have we reached the modern part of the seminary? These buildings look brand new," said Elly.

"Well, that one—the Campus Center—was built when I was here, and we got us a real pretty chapel inside. You want to see it?"

"Are you sure?"

"Of course! I've been in it many times, and have yet to burst into flames!"

"Ohh, tres modern, but homey," said Elly, walking around and inspecting the piano and massive organ. "Lutherans aren't ostentatious unless it comes to their—I hate to say it—pipe organs!"

"Ha! ha! Good. You don't like it, but that's okay." said Zara.

"Well, I grew up in an old church founded by Italian immigrants. Talk about medieval. It was brimming over with statues, crucifixes, stations of the cross, and assorted holy bric-à-brac. This is sparse, but the lighting is warm, and it feels cozy. Let's sit."

"Holy heck," said Zara, pushing her fingers through her hair and nodding. "Elly, what am I supposed to do? I mean, I can't change the past."

"Who says?" said Elly.

"What?" said Zara. "Like time-travel!? Oh, Elly!"

"Well, keep an open mind now," said Elly. "Do you remember when I was studying with that Medicine Woman, Sarah Whiterabbit, from up north?"

"Yeah," said Zara. "Well, only sort of. When you talked about it, I kind of checked out."

"You should have listened because Sarah used to talk about going into the past and changing it. She even had a ritual," said Elly.

"So, we go back into the past and prevent the *Eastland*? Come on! How can that happen with a historical event? Even a forgotten one," said Zara.

"Not quite like. Sarah used to say that all events happen over and over," said Elly. "As in a parallel universe."

"Let's say the *Eastland* Disaster 'happens' every year on July 24," said Zara. "How would I intervene? How could I jump through a time portal!?"

"Well, you'll never know until you go there—on July 24. You will return to Chicago on that day, trace Martha's steps, and see what happens," said Elly. "As bizarre as this sounds, you know it's right. Speaking of which, did you sense anything when you were at the disaster site?"

"Well, no," said Zara. "I mean, Pearl, and I didn't get to the site."

"Are you kidding? You have to!" said Elly. "You can't keep visiting her grave. You must see where Martha lived, and where she died."

"One thing at a time! I only had three days and was not going to drive around Chicago with Pearl flailing her arms, chanting 'the Blood of Jesus,' whenever I made a wrong turn. I needed to focus on her and her stories. These stories, El, are my stories. Besides descending from this family, I also descend from this disaster, and it affected me too, even if I knew nothing about it."

10

SO COMPELLING, THIS IS

"Zara, I'm getting pulled—or maybe strong-armed—into it, too," said Elly. "I have to pitch in and help."

Zara stood. "Can we go back to your place?" Elly nodded.

They walked back in silence.

Zara paused and watched Elly feed her cats. Anna Magnani stopped eating, looked at Zara, and jumped in her lap.

"Hey, kitty girl!" said Zara, rubbing the plump black and white cat's head. "I should have had this story my whole life, and now, in my mid-forties, I play catch-up. What if that's what's wrong with my life? I mean, not knowing the story?"

"Not 'wrong,' dear," said Elly. "What was lost was found! You uncovered something that's been streaming through your veins forever. It was like molten lava just waiting to erupt!"

"Tell me about it," said Zara.

"Now it's time to reassemble and reinterpret it your way. Something beyond an article. I know you're scared, but you have to stop slamming the brakes whenever life seems to get out of control."

"What are you talking about, Elly? I've just swallowed eighty-some years of missing history! That's a lot to digest!"

"This is hitting a nerve, kiddo, but I'm gonna keep insisting, because you have to do this. You're too far in and *must* see where Martha lived and where she died. Otherwise, it's a fragmented, uncompleted journey. Half-a-story is worse than an untold story."

"I'm not tracking," said Zara.

"You saw the grave. Good! You met with your Aunt Pearl, even better, and you wrote the article. But you must see all facets of Martha's life too. Her house, the grave, the disaster site, and the morgue are your clues."

"I saw the grave,"

"Then there's the very place where this takes place: Chicago! *My Kinda Town*! Places are actors in this drama, too—remember all those use cases we've written for those software projects? Same thing. The 'actor' can be a person, place, or thing."

Zara leaned against the sink and sighed.

"I reiterate. July 24 falls on a Saturday—the same as it did in 1915 —it is time to make this pilgrimage," said Elly.

"Only a couple months away," said Zara. "You'll come with me? Promise?"

"You bet, Zee. Let's follow Martha's steps on the anniversary of her death. That will make it complete," said Elly, taking Zara's hand. "I'm a Chicago girl, so give me the addresses, and we'll find the locations. Too bad, my folks moved to Sarasota, or else we could have stayed with them in Evanston."

"It'd be easier to stay downtown, so we'd be close to the action, but the hotel prices are out of my league. I keep checking, but they keep going up," said Zara.

"I had friends in Lisle. It's far west of the city, but a straight shot in, so that will work nicely," said Elly. "If we stay west, I can take you through the city via the scenic route. No freeways and damn tolls. Just plan on doing a lot of driving."

"Can you leave on the Thursday before? I mean, we could take our time and enjoy the journey and all that jazz," said Zara.

"You got it, dude," said Elly.

11

TRAVELING ON I-94

On Thursday morning, July 22nd, Zara and Elly loaded their bags into Zara's SUV and soon headed east on I-94 as the sun rose.

"Refresh my memory. We're on the road this early because —why?"

"I dunno," said Zara, "I just have a thing about driving at the break of day when nobody's around."

"I don't call this 'nobody.' Look at this traffic. You'd think they have something important to do," said Elly, pointing at the cars trying to exit on Century Avenue.

"It's just the 3M logjam. It'll lighten up once we're in Wisconsin."

In five minutes, they crossed the connecting bridge in Hudson over the scenic St. Croix River—nearly traffic-free.

"Wisconsin's pretty, isn't it? I mean, 15 minutes out of St. Paul, and we're surrounded by rocky cliffs, rolling hills, blankets of trees, and rivers," said Zara.

"Should we stop at Micky D's for coffee?" said Elly, filing her nails.

"Yeah. I'm desperate. Even that's better than nothing,"

"True. Nothing like a wonderful coffee to an Italian," said Elly. "I sure hated it when you broke up with whatshername, CoffeeGirl!"

"CoffeeGirl was crazy!" said Zara.

"I know but look at all the free lattes and cappuccinos we scored at her little bistro," said Elly.

"Ah, that was nice," said Zara. "Still, all bad things come to an end."

"What was CoffeeGirl's name?"

"Hmm, Judy, Joan, June, Jane, a J- name, but I don't remember," said Zara.

"I remember every guy I dated, and even the one I married."

"How old were you when you got married?"

"Oh, a very young 21."

"Why'd you break up?"

"Why'd we get married is the question! I grew up with Dominic, and both of our parents coerced us. There was constant pressure to be married when I was growing up—at least for Italian girls of my generation. He and I called it a day after a year, but we're still buddies, and I think he's gay."

"Oh, my! Did you ever talk about it with him?" said Zara.

"No," said Elly. "And I'm not sure even he knows, but I think I'm right."

"And what's with your parents pushing you into marriage? Don't they kind of hate each other?"

"Oh yeah, but that doesn't matter. They've been married for 60 years!"

They drove along for another hour when Zara noticed the sign for Eau Claire. "Do you mind? There's something else I want to see. It's only a bit out of the way."

"You're driving, so let's take a detour. Where do you want to go?"

"Feel like checking out Falling Brook, Wisconsin?"

12

A STOP ON THE WAY

"**O**h, yeah. Falling Brook. I've been there!" said Elly.

"You haven't!"

"About three years ago, I was antiquing in Falling Brook when a surprise blizzard hit. Within 15 minutes, we went through all four seasons! The road was glare ice and my LaCrosse skated into a ditch, but some nice farmers towed me out," said Elly. "It's a tiny town. I mean *tiny*! The main drag was probably about two blocks. So how does Falling Brook factor into your Chicago family?"

"Falling Brook is where my great-great-grandmother and most of her children lived. My great-grandparents were the only outliers since they ended up in Chicago," said Zara.

"This keeps getting weirder. Tell me you are tracking the synchronicities between you and these ancestor people. The deeper you go, the more freaked out I get!"

"How do you think I feel!? I returned to the mothership!"

"You know how much I love legends of the unexplained? There are countless reports of people drawn to places where they've never been. And then the location turned out to be significant—either in a family history or past life," said Elly.

"You lost me," said Zara.

"Let me finish! The places often turn out to be a nexus—a source of spiritual power for the seeker. Always seemed like a fun, but far-fetched, idea, but your unfolding drama is rivaling anything I've read in *Fate* magazine," said Elly.

"I promise I will never make fun of you again for reading all those new age and self-help books. But why have you stayed with me through this?"

"Should I remind you I'm Italian? Loyalty to friends is part of me being me, and you are my closest friend."

"That means the world."

"I'm one lucky girl. I mean, if I can't experience the supernatural directly, you're letting me get close."

"I'm glad you're not doing this out of obligation."

"Come on! Would I be here if I didn't want to? Change of topic. I've been wondering about reincarnation."

"In what sense?"

"Meaning you could be a reincarnation or incarnation of Martha," said Elly.

"You lost me again, and I don't..."

"Think about it. The same DNA, and that's a scientific fact. Her horrific departure shook up that bloodline, backward and forward."

"Come back from left field, please."

"I know it's a cliché, but a person who died young, or who died violently, sometimes lingers. This blithe spirit is both inside and outside of you."

"That's not as wackadoo as it sounds," said Zara.

"Told ya. Pearl's family history is the vehicle that Martha rode to make her way to you."

"I know nothing about reincarnation."

"You don't need to. You paid attention to Martha, welcomed her into your life, and now, she's returning the favor,. She's introduced you to the ancestors on this massive branch of your family tree. They're a source of strength."

"Could be."

"When the newness wears off, this will be grafted into your being. Someday, you'll feel that you've always known the story," said Elly.

13

SMALL TOWN, USA

"How did you get so wise?" said Zara.

Elly laughed. "Ah, I've always known things, but I keep them to myself. But hey, I want to ask you something else."

"Shoot," said Zara.

"Why did most of your grandmother's family end up here while your great-grandparents and their kids relocated to Chicago? That's quite a distance, and not just geographically. Talk about extremes— from a small, rural village to one of the country's largest and most industrialized cities! Literally, worlds apart. Why'd they split off?" said Elly.

"Pearl said the entire family first immigrated from Poland to Johnstown just before the 1889 Flood. So, I couldn't blame them for uprooting again after that. But you're right—why didn't they follow one another?"

"I suppose it's not unheard of, but what drew them to their respective locations?" said Elly.

"My great-grandfather's sister and family went to Chicago first. Why? I don't know, but he and his family followed his sister and her family. Maybe city life promised wealth, and the country life seemed like more backbreaking labor. My great-grandfather was a black-smith, but I don't know where in Chicago he worked."

"What about the rest of your grandmother's family?"

"I'm guessing they already knew people in Wisconsin. Maybe other family members had already settled there. I was just reading about this thing called 'chain migration' where groups of people settled in places where relatives or friends had previously settled."

"Makes sense," said Elly. "My ancestors followed other family members to Chicago in the late 1800s and ended up living in—guess where? Little Italy. Well, the good news is small towns don't change much, so did you try contacting anyone in Falling Brook?" said Elly.

"I found a cousin who's in his eighties and still living there. And I bet there are more relatives too. After all, my great-grandmother had at least six brothers and sisters who settled in that area," said Zara.

"Did you call this cousin?" said Elly.

"Uh-uh. I didn't want to risk scaring him, not after what happened with Uncle Eddie."

DRIVING THROUGH EAU CLAIRE, the landscape became moderately citified again, with the University of Wisconsin, various strip malls, motels, and fast-food emporiums. Then, as they continued along Highway 12, the terrain abruptly and majestically transformed. Laden corn and alfalfa fields enveloped the land, and the shimmering, rolling hills hedged them in.

"Jeez, these back roads are gorgeous! This is so American Gothic —blankets of cornfields, and the red barns and silos," said Elly.

"A pleasant break from concrete, yes?" said Zara as they dipped into a small valley where the lush blue-green trees momentarily obscured the morning sun.

They saw the sign "Welcome to Falling Brook: Population 1010" and an adjacent sign was a welcome from its churches.

"Holy hell! What's with all the churches? Eleven—no twelve—for a thousand people? At least half of them are Lutheran. And look!

Crabby Bob's Tavern! All you can eat!" said Elly, pointing to a bar on the northeast corner of the block that was the main street. "And there's another bar right next to it!"

Zara laughed. "Yeah, we're in the heart of Leinenkugel country. Probably not much to do here other than drink, go to church, and repent."

"Park the car and let's check this out," said Elly.

They parked in the street in front of a bank and started walking.

"Look at these buildings. This is like a movie backlot for a Western. All that's missing are the wooden sidewalks."

"It is kind of other-worldly. So unpretentious and functional—and nothing is here to impress. Do you know how some small towns work hard at being cute and charming? Well, this ain't one of them," said Zara.

"Just like you!" laughed Elly.

Along with the two taverns, the main street included one library, a community hall, bank, and a feed store built in various indeterminate styles—including quasi-Swiss Chalet, white clapboard, and painted-over brick. No building was over three stories high.

"It's amazing that there are still places like this in America. Small towns around the Twin Cities were devoured by suburban development," said Zara. "But places like this seem to have intentionally stopped changing long ago, and I love that! Still, I wonder why? Even if you wanted to restore it, what would you restore it to?"

"Places like Stillwater and Red Wing have those inviting red brick buildings. Creates the illusion of an uncluttered, simple past and attracts tourists. Not this place. I like Falling Brook's attitude."

14

MORE THAN MEETS THE EYE

"First stop. Trinity Cemetery," said Zara.

"I see the sign. Turn left," said Elly.

They parked on the gravel road in front of the cemetery.

"Bless Pearl forever and ever. She took a photo of my great-great grandmother's grave so I think I can find it," said Zara.

"Let me see," said Elly. "It's right in front of a shed."

Zara looked up and pointed. "There's the shed."

They stood in front of the stone—no larger than a brick. The word "Mother" was nearly unreadable.

"Every family needs an Aunt Pearl. Without this photo and note, you wouldn't know who this is," said Elly.

"You said it," said Zara.

"Your great-great grandmother's grave! I'd have to fly to Sicily to see anyone that far back in my family. Aren't you thrilled? I am," said Elly.

"I'm numb. New day, new discovery. I can keep up with it—intellectually. But my emotions—that's where I feel lost."

"It takes time. You'll figure how this puzzle piece fits into your life."

"Once upon a time, I had a rigid idea of what—and who—I came from."

"You angry?"

"Maybe. But who to be angry with? It's no one's fault."

"Say, can I see Pearl's notes again?"

"Sure," said Zara.

"Your great-great grandmother was Marie Stra--? Umm. How is that last name pronounced?"

"Straw-shin-skee," said Zara. "Don't feel bad. It took me a few tries to get it right."

"Born in 1837! Wowser. That was before the Civil War!" said Elly.

"Had she been born in America, she would have witnessed that!" said Zara.

"I've never thought of you as a Polish person before," said Elly.

"Me, either."

"Is that upsetting? If I found I was something other than Sicilian in my background, I..."

"I didn't have a sense of a single ethnic identity."

"You're kidding! Did no one talk about where they came from?"

"Sure! My mom's dad lived with us and swore he was German— but I never bought that completely. Mom never challenged him and proclaimed us German—forgetting my dad's parents were from Czechoslovakia."

"Families are so strange," said Elly.

"Hold on! It gets better. After Grandpa died, I found his naturalization papers. He was born in Poland! He considered himself an ethnic German, but never lived in Germany. So, both of Mom's parents were from what is now Poland, but was probably part of Prussia then. I never explored that further since I distanced myself from her family—until now. Always identified with my dad's people and felt this deep bond with being Slovak and Rusyn."

"Russian?"

"No. Rusyn and it is pronounced *roos-in* maybe to distinguish it from Russian. Rusyns are an ethnic group—a stateless people—who live in eastern Slovakia, and parts of Poland and Ukraine. But that's another discussion," said Zara.

"Oh please. One confusing thing at a time! So, back when your grandfather and mom tried to cancel out your dad's side—you did a counter-cancel on them."

"Is counter-cancel a thing?"

"It is now. Ethnic Germans in Poland? I'm no expert, but that Straw...ski surname sounds very Polish. And this other group—Rusyns. You're even more complex than I realized."

"I'm gonna figure out how to make a family tree and maybe deep dive into Eastern European history."

"I never thought of what it would be like to navigate multiple ethnicities in one's background. Which one do you pay attention to? How do you identify yourself?" said Elly.

Zara said nothing.

Elly paused and said, "What a twist of fate. What it would have been like had your great-grandparents moved here instead of Chicago? I mean, Martha would have never been on the *Eastland* and your grandmother might have never died so young."

"I might have never been born! Can't imagine living in a small town since I'd mostly lived in bigger cities. I thought Johnstown was a small town..."

"Johnstown," said Elly, snapping her fingers. "The Flood!"

"Yeah," said Zara, "You know that! Remember. My great-grandfather's sister was in the Flood of 1889, only she was rescued."

SORRY, kiddo. My brain can't keep up with all of this, but holy hell!" said Elly, "Two major disasters and you have relatives in each? What does it mean?"

"What could it possibly mean, except some of us are in the wrong place at the wrong time!"

"Remind me never to go on a cruise with you!" said Elly. "Nah. There are no coincidences. It means something. It's connected, of that I'm sure. Souls travel in packs, and they each agree to carry out specific missions."

"What are you talking about?"

"You know about Elisabeth Kubler-Ross?"

"Sure. *Death and Dying*," said Zara.

"You know how she got into her work?"

"I guess I'm going to in a second."

They sat on the grass near a circle of other gravestones, and Elly talked while the birds and crickets bade them good morning.

"This has everything to do with you," said Elly. "This happened early in her career at the University of Chicago. Chicago again! Well, she was getting a lot of crap from colleagues about her death and dying work and was ready to throw in the towel. She took the elevator to her office to pack up when she saw a woman waiting for her. Someone who looked familiar."

"And..." said Zara.

"It was a former patient—someone who had died! And this dead woman returned to tell Kubler-Ross to continue her work," said Elly.

"I heard she went wacko toward the end," said Zara.

"I repeat, this was at the beginning of her career," said Elly. "She wrote about it in her book, *On Life After Death*."

"Oh, that's hard to believe," said Zara.

"Why? You're living a variation of it!" said Elly.

"What do you mean? I have seen no one—not that I want to," said Zara.

"But you have! Zara, I'd sell my eyeteeth to be in your shoes! I'd love to see my Zia Teresa again."

"No, you wouldn't!" said Zara.

"What?? Of course, I would! Why does this upset you so?"

"Elly, I didn't ask for this," said Zara, chewing on a blade of grass. "I don't want to hunt ghosts, attend Edgar Cayce conventions, or have past-life regressions. I don't need one more damn anything that makes me different."

"Well, why are you doing this, then? Explain, or we won't enjoy this trip."

"I'm sorry El, I am. It's a pressure I feel all the time now. I'm scared," said Zara.

"Explain!"

Zara said, "It's bad enough being gay in this society. Now to pile on being psychic or whatever this is! God, Elly, my life was fine, and I miss my carnal side, but I can't do it anymore. It's lost its pull. When I go on dates now, I'm bored."

Zara continued, "What started as a research project turned into a Pandora's Box! I used to think it was impossible to be more of a misfit than I am, but here we are!"

"So, if it's so hard, why do you continue?" asked Elly. "Why?"

"Because it's relentless. The Call. If you want to give it a name. The more I ignore it, the stronger it becomes. When I try ducking it, I feel out of sync. Aw, shit, I'm too much in my head when I try explaining it—and believe me, it's not my head that's pulling me. It's hooked my heart."

15

WHO'S CHOOSING WHO?

"Okay. We should probably go," said Zara. She bowed before the grave, kissed her fingertips, and then touched her great-great grandmother's gravestone.

"When we get back from Chicago, you need to come back here. There's more here than meets the eye."

"Agree. There's something about this little place. I'm kind of in love with it," said Zara.

～

THEY REACHED the Lisle Days Inn just past 7:00 p.m.

"It's stifling hot!" said Zara, parking the car.

"Chicago's always hot in the summer. Miserable. Let's check in, unpack, have showers and find an Italian restaurant," said Elly.

～

"DAMN IT!" said Zara, sniffing the room. "I asked for nonsmoking!"

"Well, the price is right, don't worry."

"You shower first. I want to write a bit."

~

July 23, 1999. Tomorrow is the anniversary of the Eastland Disaster. I must be there. Will you be there, too? Will I be able to reach back in time, pluck you out, and save you? Can I stop the Eastland Disaster by being there 84 years later? Of course not! Yet, by walking with you, our lives will be changed. Forever. This, I know.

I will not be commemorating. Instead, I will step into your being, retrace your steps, reenact the whole day, and walk the sacred labyrinth. Will you show your face again? If I match your actions precisely at the same time on the same date, what will happen?

Maybe I will rage at the Chicago River for taking you, for shattering my grandmother's heart, for leaving my mother motherless, and for abandoning me.

I was robbed! We all were, and I have returned to reclaim what was ours

.

~

ZARA CRINGED when she heard Elly call her name.

"Oh, sorry, Zee! You want to continue writing?" said Elly.

"I'm done," said Zara, closing the notebook.

"Let's get vino rosa and pasta," said Elly. "I can live off the memories when we return to Saint Paul. Why, oh, why, is there no decent Italian restaurant in the Twin Cities?"

"On the way back, let's stop at a florist," said Zara. "I want to buy a rose and throw it in the river tomorrow."

"I'll get one too," said Elly. "I want to remember her, too, and tell her how much I like her half-crazed grandniece."

~

THE NEXT DAY, the women started early.

"Martha probably left around 5:30 a.m., so maybe we can get to her house around then," said Elly.

"Let's do it," said Zara, securing her seatbelt. "Are you sure you can find it?"

"Yeah, 2708 West 23rd Street," said Elly, staring at the MapQuest directions. It's off Cermak. Did your Aunt Pearl tell you about the neighborhood? I mean, she lived there too as a child."

"Mostly, Polish and German immigrants back then," said Zara. "I learned, though, that Chicago, back then, was a rough place. I mean, crime was unbelievable."

"And that's different how?" said Elly.

"It seemed worse. The gist of Sandburg's *Eastland* poem was that he saw a hundred '*Eastlands*' on his way to work each day. So, in his eyes, the entire city, at least the working classes, was filled with disaster."

"Chicago was always a mix of seedy and spectacular," said Elly. "So much for the good old days, but I love it!"

"Oh, yes," said Zara. "It's magnificent."

"Turn here. No wait, do a U-ee," said Elly, leading them down a street off Ogden.

"Spanish is now the mother tongue, eh?" said Zara, pointing to the storefronts.

"From one set of immigrants to the next," said Elly. "Oh, quick, Zara, here's the street."

Turning down West 23rd Street they slowed and counted the house numbers until they saw the small two-story home.

"That's it," said Zara. "Twenty-seven zero eight."

Parking proved a chore, but they squeezed in between two vehicles.

They stood in front of the home, getting as close as they could without being intrusive.

"How old is it?" said Elly, getting her camera.

"Pearl said it was built around 1895. So, it was pretty new when my family moved here in the early 1900s."

Zara stared at the maroon brick dwelling with the ridiculous AstroTurf-ed green front steps, wishing she could go inside.

How did they cram everyone into such a tiny place?

The narrow, unevenly spaced windows gave it a dollhouse appearance, and the houses on either side were practically stacked on top of one another.

If she spoke Spanish, she might have knocked on the door and asked to come inside, but she didn't and she wouldn't. And she certainly didn't want to frighten the occupants. She also felt queasy remembering Pearl's tales of Ruthie, the last relative to live there. The house was in shambles after Ruthie and her many cats were forced out.

She wished the abode would break its chilly silence and spill its secrets instead of staring her down.

Zara stood where her ancestors once stood. Maybe they were still going on about their business—their ghosts walking right through her. She planted her feet and bent her knees slightly, assuming a martial arts stance in front of the house.

She needed to anchor herself, for she stood on sacred ground. Martha departed this place 84 years before—on another fateful Saturday, on another July 24. Despite the heat and humidity, Zara was freezing.

She felt a sudden energy surge, and nonstop shivers ricocheted up and down her spine. Then came the now-familiar caresses of the invisible fingertips. Her legs felt wobbly.

She focused on the uppermost window—probably the bedroom that Uncle Eddie wrote about—where he, Martha, Ida, and Louisa slept when they were children.

She glanced at Elly, who was still engrossed in her photography.

"How about I get some shots of the other side of the street? You don't know where Judge Stelk lived—the one who employed Martha as his housekeeper?"

"No, but those houses across the street look more stately," said Zara.

Elly snapped more photos. Some neighbors walked by, but no one paid them any attention.

"So, Martha started from here," said Elly. "And do you know where she picked up the streetcar?"

"No," said Zara. "It could have been as close as the next block. Chicago had more streetcars than any city in the country back then."

"This is something," said Elly. "I'm so glad we're here! Anything else you want me to photograph?"

"No, let's get to the disaster site," said Zara. Both women were silent as they walked to the car.

~

"WHICH WAY?"

"Go to the end of the street, then turn right."

"Elly, when we were standing in front of the house, I felt something, I felt..."

"...Fingers gently caressing your arms," said Elly.

Zara gasped.

"Yeah, I felt it too. It was so sweet. I think they know I'm taking care of you on this journey. Oh Zara," said Elly, her eyes filling with tears.

"What?" said Zara.

"Oh, kiddo! You really opened the door to something, and please don't doubt that," said Elly.

"I don't. I feel so many things. No words. Just untranslatable emotions." Driving under a maze of iron beams, Zara asked, "What's that?"

"The underbelly of the El," said Elly.

"Chicago is raw nerve endings. Even before I knew anything about my family history, I felt Chicago was watching me whenever I visited. No other city affected me like this. A combination of being unnerved but drawn to it."

Elly said, "Now you know why."

"Quite a dramatic bunch—my family."

"Okay, slow down. We're almost there, and I always get lost with these one-ways. We can take Wacker all the way in. Get off on Congress, yeah, that's right."

"Gad, there's this loopy-loop thing," said Zara, turning the car. "What makes it north and south? The streets, I mean?"

"I think it has to do with the relationships to the Loop—the downtown business district—and the El. The intersection of Madison and State—South Loop Northside, West Side, it's all in how it's related to the Loop," said Elly. "This is it."

As they pulled up on Wacker between Clark and LaSalle, Zara recognized the site.

"There it is, Elly, the factory," said Zara, pointing to the Reid Murdoch Building across the street. "Just the same as in the old photos. There it is. There it is."

They parked in the pay lot across the street, got out of the car and stared.

"Come on, let's get close," said Elly.

Walking across the street, they stood on the bridge looking over the Chicago River. On a perfect weather day, the blue waves cascaded languidly as if they hadn't a care in the world.

"It looks just the way it did," said Zara.

16

FLOWER IN THE RIVER

"You needed to see all of this, however painful. Web pages, letters, and photographs alone will not take you where you need to go emotionally," said Elly.

Zara stared at the ground and mumbled, "You're right, but I'm sick of emotions that I can't describe."

"So, do you feel anything?" said Elly.

"Nothing I can describe. Standing so close to where she died makes it real," said Zara.

Staring at the Chicago River below, she shook her head. "This space is so tight. How did it hold a gigantic ship along with thousands of onlookers?"

"Maybe they've done some reconstruction since 1915," said Elly.

"Except the Reid Murdoch Building looks about the same," said Zara. "Have you noticed something odd?"

"Besides what?" said Elly.

"Other than the handful of passersby, there's no one here on the anniversary of Chicago's *Titanic*. Just us. Not even a friggin' wreath or memorial."

"It's as if it never happened," said Elly.

They wandered down the slight hill to the river's edge.

Zara said, "The river looks so serene now, but can you imagine what it was like at the turn of the century?"

"Chicago definitely had some major sanitation problems. And the river was a Petri dish of sorts. All kinds of disease outbreaks happened in the 1900s," said Elly.

"I heard all the stories. I don't think we can fathom now what Chicago was back then. The world looked at it as a symbol of American progress," said Zara.

"It was a happening place for sure. The World's Columbian Exposition was a big, big deal. The museums, the architecture...."

"The industrialization, the stockyards and, oh, the books. *The Jungle, Sister Carrie,* and *Native Son*—were staples of American lit, that's a fact."

"And our friend, Sandburg's 'Chicago, Hog Butcher of the world' poem."

"Always an odd mix of opulence and poverty. And it's where our immigrant ancestors cut their teeth," said Zara

"Get the flowers," said Elly.

Zara removed the two wilted red roses from her backpack and gave Elly one.

"You first, Zee," said Elly.

"Aunt Martha, I'm here. I told you I would be here to remember you," said Zara. "I'm so sorry. I'm sorry! I..." And she sobbed.

Elly put her arm around Zara's shoulder and said, "Beautiful and forever-young Martha! I likewise honor you. Thank you for letting me share this journey with Zara. This rose is small and delicate, just like your life. Yet, we've seen that a flower in the river has powerful ripples that extend beyond time and this catastrophe. We remember you. We honor you."

Both women dropped their roses into the Chicago River.

"You okay, kid?" said Elly.

Zara nodded. "I'm fine, but I'll never be okay. Not ever. Everything is different now."

"Even I can't wrap my mind around this. We, um, both need time to absorb everything," said Elly.

Walking back up the hill, they saw it. A small *Eastland* memorial plaque mounted on a pole and obscured by overgrown bushes.

"Nice! Just this insignificant little plaque!" said Elly.

"This is a goddamn insult! Along with the dead, they also buried the disaster," said Zara, while they examined the plaque.

"Ugh," said Zara. "The print is so faded that it's hard to read."

"Well, take heart. The *Eastland* Disaster won't stay lost permanently. Look at how quickly your article took off, and your little paper's not even online," said Elly.

"Maybe it was fortunate that it was hidden all this time," said Zara.

"The memorial plaque?" said Elly.

"The disaster! If it were well-known, the ghouls would have swarmed in like vultures. If anyone sniffs another *Titanic* story, they'll try to make a buck off it. You know that."

"Look, Zara," said Elly, "no one else has your unique family history, and that's for all eternity. It's yours. But if only that river could talk to us."

"Who says it can't?"

"What do you mean?" said Elly, as they both leaned against the fence for one last look at the river.

"What does water do? It's a mirror, it reflects—its nature is to reflect," said Zara.

"Now, who's sounding new-agey?" said Elly.

"It's science," said Zara. "My mother would probably ask 'what are the properties of water?' Perhaps a large-scale tragedy gets photocopied—by nature and by the buildings that witnessed it."

"Weirdly, that makes sense," said Elly.

"And there was something you said back in Wisconsin," said Zara.

"About what?" said Elly.

"The Johnstown Flood. My Aunt Julia was in the Flood but rescued and Aunt Martha was crushed and buried underwater. Water. Luther's Catechism said something like 'baptized into death and rise into new life.' Water and baptism. And holy communion deals with blood," said Zara. "These practices refer to rituals that were much older than Christianity. Timeless, maybe."

"Blood is thicker than water," said Elly.

"Could the blood, like water, remember?" Zara said.

"Well, your blood certainly remembers. Fact is, your mind has been your biggest hurdle on this trip, and you know exactly what I mean. The Force runs strong in your family!" said Elly.

"Well, it's not a literal baptism, but a baptism, where, this time, I'm charged with bringing a life, a history from the water."

"Well, are you ready to go to the morgue site?"

"Yeah, Elly. I'm ready," said Zara. "Let me look at my directions. It's on West Washington Boulevard, and the cross streets are Carpenter and Aberdeen. Unfortunately, this won't be an exact match since a section of the armory was torn down years ago, so I doubt this will look anything like the photos."

17

OPRAH'S STUDIOS?

The drive from the disaster site was quick, and they soon found themselves in front of the Second Regiment Armory site. They stared. Gape-mouthed.

Zara leaned into the steering wheel, pressing her head against the windshield.

"Have mercy! Is this the right address?"

"Yes!! The map just left out this—uh—little detail! But this is it."

"This trip just got weirder. Well, seeing is believing!"

"Oprah's studios! My personal goddess! The big O! She puts the "O" in Omigod! Her studio is on the same block as the armory!"

"Look at that sign! *The Oprah Winfrey Show*. How many times did I rush home to catch her show?"

"A lot! That's why I bought you that damn VCR!" said Elly. "Did Oprah know where she built her studio?"

"She must have. So, we can add Oprah to the *Eastland* story. Never saw that coming."

"I'm losing track of all the rabbit holes we've slithered down. Shoot! I wish it was open so we could see it," said Elly.

They ambled around the building, which seemed more citadel than studio.

"Still looks like an armory to me," said Zara.

"Same building, with major renovations, I bet. Harpo Studios—formerly the Second Regiment Armory and morgue for the *Eastland* victims," said Elly. "Go figure."

"Well, Oprah is not just any talk-show host, but a force. She's the spiritual director for the world," said Zara.

"There's no one like her, that's for sure."

"But she's reworked the space by filling it with life. Now that's a lesson on how to deal with tragedy."

"How many lives have been changed for the better because of what happens inside Harpo Studios—a former receptacle of death."

"Isn't that the truth? *Mein gott*, my head hurts. Well, there was also a nightclub on this spot, and I think it's that restaurant across the street," said Zara.

Elly said, "Well, this cross street may not have existed in 1915. The original armory probably extended from Harpo to where the night-club-restaurant is now. We'd need a map from that period to see what it looked like. Time travel is making me hungry, so how about breakfast?"

They were the sole patrons inside the restaurant, a lovely Art Deco-like structure with exposed brick and plants.

"This is the first normal thing we've done this morning," said Zara.

"Uhh, no. We're eating where all those dead bodies once were."

"Oh thanks," said Zara.

"Can you imagine the chaos that engulfed the city that day? I can't." said Elly. "And here we are, having a leisurely, civilized breakfast."

"Great food," said Zara. "A girl has to eat, and these eggs are excellent."

"We're near Little Italy, you know," said Elly. "But there's not much to it anymore. Greektown is still going strong, though. Pepsi! Pepsi! Pepsi!"

Zara laughed, "Coke! Coke! Coke!"

"Zara! Check-in time again. Do you feel anything close to what we felt back at the house?"

"Elly, my circuits are overloaded. Oprah!? What comes after that? But the house has been the most, well, kinetic, part of this journey," said Zara.

"I wonder why the house had so much energy—since I expected more vibes from the disaster site."

"It's impossible to predict what will—what won't—happen on this little venture," said Zara.

They boxed the rest of breakfast, squared up the bill, and headed out the door.

ELLY SAID, "To Bethania Cemetery, we go!"

"I know the way," said Zara.

They were mostly quiet while driving toward Archer Avenue.

"Oh, I love this part of town. So close to the Forest Preserve," said Elly.

"I'll never forget my first visit. I did not expect such an idyllic setting, especially so close to the city," said Zara, pulling into the gates of Bethania.

Elly said, "I forgot that I have some family members buried right next door."

"Resurrection Cemetery?" said Zara.

"My, oh my! You have learned your cemeteries well," said Elly. "And I did some homework too and learned that Bethania was the Protestant cemetery in this area—founded in 1894. Martha and your other family members might have been some of its earliest residents if that's the right word."

"Right," said Zara. "I read that a bell would toll whenever there was a funeral. How many times did it chime when this happened?"

"The bell ringer must have lost his upper-range hearing after that," said Elly.

They exited the car and made their way toward the Pfeiffer headstones. Elly exclaimed, "Oh! Your family's headstones are gorgeous! Much larger than I thought they'd be. They were costly and even the inscription, *Auf die Eastland*, must have cost a pretty penny."

"You're right. Hard to tell how they were set up after my great-grandfather's death, but they seemed to be neither rich nor poor."

"This is so charming, and I could stay here all day! People used to picnic in cemeteries, y'know. Not sure where the aversion to death started."

"My mom remembered her own mother's body laid out in their living room. This was 1934 when Mom was just three. She said they placed bouquets on the steps to alert people that someone inside had died."

"We grew up with funeral homes, but maybe they were smarter back then. Having the dearly departed in the home kept it real."

"Well, let's sit and have a picnic," said Zara.

"Why not?" said Elly. "I think your family will welcome the company. Let me get the coffee and the rest of our breakfast from the car."

They sat under the tree next to the family headstones.

"I feel as if we're visiting them," said Elly.

"I know! The first time, I cried buckets when I realized I'd parked right in front of their graves and didn't know it. I was so shattered that morning, but sensed they were welcoming me."

"Ahh, so lovely," said Elly. "I'm glad they reciprocated, and I bet they appreciated your trying."

"Ha! By then, I felt coerced," said Zara.

"Listen—when those genetic rumblings amplified, you could have stifled them, but you opened the door," said Elly.

"At heart, I am a journalist, and curiosity upstages fear," said Zara.

"True, but there's more to it," smiled Elly. "I think you're wired to be a receptacle for all things paranormal."

"Weird. Huh?"

"You were born that way, and don't make a joke! This is tough for me to wrap my mind around."

"How so?"

"Well, I have to get used to a new you, for one thing. We've known each other for over ten years, and we've been through so much together. Yet, there were so many parts of you that I never knew. I guess because you never knew."

"It seems like yesterday when I sauntered into your office for that interview. So, why'd you hire me in the first place?"

"I dunno," said Elly. "You were rather cocky back then, but you had the intelligence and inquisitiveness that the company lacked. I thought you could help revive it. And you spent time with Brian. My other staff were cordial to him but kept a distance—I'm guessing because the cerebral palsy made it hard to understand him."

"Oh, Brian! May he rest in peace," said Zara. "He wasn't hard to understand—you just had to listen. We shared a warped sense of humor too! And, after you hired me, he was my go-to person for all things network-related. I used to call him 'Brian the Brain!'"

"That's what I mean. You saw the person, not the disability," said Elly.

"I just liked him," said Zara.

"Yes, indeedy," said Elly, taking Zara's hands. "That brings us to now. I have to know you all over again. This expedition has turned my belief system on its axis."

"Your belief system? Explain!"

"Well, I'd always hoped there was an afterlife. I hoped our dead loved ones would continue caring for us, but all I had was hope. And then all...this. That takes me to a crossroads, too, so maybe I need to put my money where my mouth is."

"What do you mean?"

"Well, you weren't much of a believer in any sense, and look at you now! You're slowly and deliberately opening yourself up to another view of reality. Your confidence is growing, and you're not so self-conscious and apologetic. Of course, it's petty, but I'm jealous since that used to be my domain!"

"Not exactly, Elly. I experienced the unexplained so often when I was a kid. I grew up surrounded by a grandmother who referred to herself as 'La Strega' and various aunts and cousins who were deep into folk magic."

"La Strega?! That's Italian for witch! What the heck?"

"Johnstown had lots of Italian immigrants, too, so maybe that's where she picked it up. And she embraced her Strega-ness."

"So, why did you distance yourself from it?"

"Life happened," said Zara. "Reality, as defined by the overarching culture, happened. My years in various churches didn't help either, since the only 'magic' the church folks allowed was curated by them. The magic words over the bread and wine, for example. Everything else was 'of the devil.' So, the dominant culture won. And I boxed away the childish machinations of my enchanted childhood, never thinking I'd embrace that again."

"And now, you have come full circle," said Elly. *"Will the Circle Be Unbroken?"*

*T*HE *BLOOD REMEMBERS what the mind never knew.*

18

JUST PASSING THROUGH

Their Chicago visit marked a significant milestone: a completed research mission.

"What do you want to do?" asked Elly.

"Nothing. I mean, this was a life-changing trip, but all journeys end," said Zara.

"End? There ya go again. Getting scared, applying the brakes. Stop it!"

Zara crossed her arms and stood up straight. "I'm not!"

"You are! This is hardly an end," said Elly. "Just a pause. Time to catch your breath. God. You are annoying sometimes, though."

"Annoying? Look. I'm grateful. I couldn't have navigated without you, Elly. And I don't mean the driving part. But I've done nearly everything that I wanted: written an article, checked out Falling Brook, visited Aunt Pearl, and now retraced Martha's steps? So, what remains?" said Zara.

"This is not a checklist kind of thing. You tell me what remains?" said Elly.

"No. I'm turning the tables—what about YOU?"

"Me? this is about you!"

"It's not. Remember what I asked before? Once this little detour is over, how about we start a new company? I know you've been thinking about it. Our current company is on life support, in case you need a reminder."

"Back to that again? Do I need to remind you of what happened at Quest when we..."

"Now, who's applying the brakes? Yeah, we lost everything. But if it's just us, we could do things better. Our way."

"Well, if we do, promise you'll do the hiring!"

"Me?"

"Remember Cranky Judy, our so-called HR manager? She was awful—nasty, bitter, and just blah. But after her bad hires—and a few of your snarky *I told you so's*—she asked you to do early candidate reconnaissance," said Elly.

"I forgot! Judy had me walk through the lobby when we had an applicant and report my impressions. After that, she never made a hire unless I felt good about it. And, as I recall, all my hires worked out," said Zara.

"See? What'd I tell you?" said Elly.

"Living people are easy to read! It's a bit different with the dead," said Zara.

"Is it? What we call 'living people' is tantamount to energy inhabiting a meat skeleton, putting it crudely. You're not reading body language. You're reading their life force, their vibration," said Elly.

"But so what? It's not as if we can make communication with the dead into a business."

"Not directly, but we could use your intuition and sleuthing to help people and, in turn, help us."

"You mean, like a private investigator?"

"A very unique private investigative service. I'll admit I've been thinking about this. Just didn't want to say anything yet. I can see it."

"You're not kidding, are you?"

"Dead serious if you pardon the expression. I'm a born entrepreneur and went from success to success—until we bombed out at Quest. Now, I'm getting charged up again."

"What do we do?"

"We do what we've been doing, and then grow it out. You just solved an eighty-odd-year-old cold case with your investigative prowess."

"It wasn't a cold case."

"Not in the technical sense, but it was a case that had grown cold. A tremendous injustice that faded into oblivion and needed resurrection. You dug up the body, put life into her, and named the perpetrators. When you apply your no-holds-barred focus on a task, there's no stopping you. You're like a pig digging for truffles!"

"Excuse me?"

"Okay. You're like a dog with a bone. You're relentless, and you don't stop until you solve the problem at hand. That, my friend, is what an investigator does. Part art. Part science."

"It's nothing special. It just came naturally."

"To you, yes. Among other things, you're strategic—probably related to your extreme intuition. I don't think that can be taught."

Zara tilted her head and looked at the ceiling.

"Look here. A little about *my* blood. I come from a long line of successful business-people. True. A few were on the other side of the law, but we don't talk about that," said Elly.

"As long as you don't have me following people around in my car and taking their photos."

"Don't jump the gun just yet. I'm seeing possibilities. Not ready for a business plan yet, but I can see it on the horizon. So, we will be methodical about this."

"Who thought this up in the first place?"

"You brought it up."

"I was just thinking of a training company, not a whole new line of business."

"Should I remind you that we signed iron-clad non-competes and they will go after us—remember what happened to Sam? They cleaned him out."

"How could I forget?"

"Well, noodle on it, but this suddenly feels so right."

"Still, before we do that, there's something else. Remember Martha?"

"Of course. Maybe we can name our new company after her!"

"Something feels odd about the timing of everything," said Zara.

"How so?" said Elly.

"Something big and not necessarily good is coming our way," said Zara.

"Right now, I can't imagine anything bad happening. The country is doing well, and even I've made money on the stock market! The world is mostly peaceful."

"I know. But in my head, I keep seeing entities beyond Martha. Almost an army of the dead, if you can imagine such a thing, here to help us,"

"Did I ever tell you—you're kind of a buzzkill?" said Elly.

"Many times," said Zara.

"The timing for our soon-to-be business might be right then. We can offer something distinctive. A just-in-time solution for people when they need it. But back to the original question—now what?" said Elly.

"Well, all this talk of investigations makes me think I need to go deeper. I want to see if any of those Falling Brook relatives will talk to me."

"What are you afraid of?"

"These are family members who don't know I exist. Until a few months ago, I didn't know they existed. So, I'm about to disrupt other lives, not just mine. Still, I'm desperate. Maybe I'll find someone who remembers Martha or my grandmother, but I won't know if I don't try," said Zara.

"You're putting a lot of pressure on yourself."

"Dealing with the living is not my forte, but there's one confession I don't want to have to utter."

"What's that?"

"From the *Book of Common Prayer*, 'We have left undone those things which we ought to have done.' I don't want to leave anything undone."[1]

"You'll accomplish everything—and more. And in the meantime, I'll start on our new business."

19

MARIAN THE LIBRARIAN IS A COUSIN OF MINE

Zara rushed to the office early to get a head-start on script reviews, and realized she needed to get corrections from her clients. She tried dialing out, only to hear that familiar sound of silence. The long-distance service was disconnected—again.

Zara flung the receiver onto the desk, shattering it into smithereens. Her heart thudded, her head pounded, and she wondered if she would spontaneously combust and end up in the *Weekly World News*.

Just then, Elly returned to their office.

"What in the hell happened to your phone?" said Elly.

"Those assholes didn't pay the bill, and so I couldn't call Dearborn! Again!" said Zara. "I lost my temper."

"You can't call anyone now!" said Elly. "You killed the phone! Oh, well. We can tell Miss Mary you dropped it."

"Don't bother," said Zara. "I'm leaving."

"For an early lunch?" asked Elly.

"No. I gotta get outta here!" said Zara. "Not coming back—well, not at least for a few days. This place is killing me, and they won't even notice I'm gone."

"Wait. Listen to me for a sec," said Elly.

Zara pounded her fists against her desk and slammed her body into the chair. "Okay," she snarled.

"You're right about starting a new business. I can't lie to myself. I've spent too much time here, and I guess inertia set in. But this company is disintegrating exponentially now. It's time," said Elly.

Zara breathed deeply and said, "I'm relieved because I can't take much more of this." Then she began loading her backpack with a writing tablet and some pens.

"Going to Chicago again?" said Elly.

"Not this time. Fancy another trip to Falling Brook?" said Zara.

"You're going to do it, eh? I'd join you if I could. God knows, I'd love to do some more antiquing, but I have to get ready for a sales call, except..." said Elly, who began dialing.

"Well?" said Zara.

"Now the local line is DOA! Oh, for the love of all things holy!" said Elly. "How are we supposed to conduct business?!"

"Two Dixie Cups and a string?" said Zara.

"Are you sure you don't want to come with?" said Zara.

"I can't let my clients down. It's not their fault this place is such a mess. I'll call them on my phone and send the bill to Stevie."

"Watch it! I tried that and gave a phone bill to Stevie last month. It has yet to be paid, and it was over one hundred dollars," said Zara.

"I forgot about that!" said Elly. "Well, I'll get cracking on a business plan. No time like the present. Go on now. Make sure not to leave anything undone."

"Catch ya later, El," said Zara. "Sorry I blew."

"Forget it. Just call when you get there, so I know you're safe," said Elly.

"All right, Mom!" said Zara.

HEADING EASTWARD ON I-94, she wondered what she'd find this time. Pearl said that she, her grandmother, and probably Martha had also taken the train from Chicago to Falling Brook in the summers. Zara never considered that various forms of transportation—trains and ships, anyway—were also significant "characters" in any family's history. What was travel like back then? Who and what did they encounter on those extended journeys?

Pearl called a few days ago to tell her that Great-Uncle Eddie, who was almost 100, died. Losing Martha's brother and only living sibling amplified her desperation and anxiety. She had to keep moving.

The timing couldn't be worse! Who am I kidding? Anyone who would have known Martha would be dead by now.

Driving down Highway 12, Zara was struck by the now familiar wide-open space, wondering what it would have been like to grow up here. The downside of city living was feeling hemmed in constantly. No chance of that here.

The darker, richer hues of the autumn sun reflected off the corn and hay bales that dotted the two-lane highway. Zara focused on the most ordinary things—trees, silos, and barns that zipped by. How many ancestors had passed through the same places?

WHO KNEW that a genealogical hotspot would come disguised as an unassuming rural village?

What do you have to teach me, Falling Brook? What can I teach you? First stop—the library.

Zara leapt out of her car and headed toward the white clapboard building. Other than the sound of the wind rustling through the trees, and screeching hawks, everything was silent. The cow manure smell took her breath away.

The wooden door creaked as she opened it. About the size of her high school study hall, the library had zero patrons and one librarian, who glared at Zara. Although they were probably close in age, the librarian appeared older, with her wire-rimmed glasses, high cheekbones, and golden-grey hair held in a tight bun. She was sporting a floral print reminiscent of an old Holly Hobby greeting card. "Marian the Librarian" from *The Music Man* immediately came to mind.

"Uh, excuse me," said Zara to the woman. "Can you help me?"

The woman said nothing but stood, watched Zara, and then began sizing her up and down. She finally said, "What do you need?"

A flummoxed Zara said, "Umm, I'm not sure exactly, but I'm looking for records for a Lutheran church."

"Which Lutheran church?" said the librarian.

"Not sure," said Zara.

"We have six Lutheran churches!" said the librarian.

"Six Lutheran churches in a town of 1,000 is—remarkable! Well, I don't know which ones, so could I look at all of them?" said Zara.

"Lots of books," said the librarian.

"Point me in the right direction, and I'll get them," said Zara.

"No. They're in the back, and I'll have to get them," said Marian.

At first, Zara wanted to apologize for asking this woman to do—well—anything. But then she asserted herself.

"I'm not trying to be rude, but I came in from the Cities to do some family research. I'm not sure where to look, but I'm a journalist and know how to hunt through stacks of books, so just let me see everything you have. Please!" said Zara.

"Which family are you researching?" asked Marian.

"I only know the ones who are below ground," said Zara.

"What are the surnames?" asked Marian.

"Hold on, let me pull out this page. Here are the names," said Zara.

"May I see?" said Marian. She read the first page and narrowed her eyes and squinted. She handed the paper back to Zara.

"Who are the Straszynski people to you?" asked Marian.

"Franz and Marie, listed at the top of the page, are my great-great-grandparents," said Zara.

"Are they, now?" said Marian.

"Do you know of them?" asked Zara.

For the first time, Marian smiled. "I should say I do since they're my great-great-grandparents, too," said Marian.

"What?!" said Zara.

"May I see your document again?" She scanned it and said, "Ah, yes! Here's my great-grandmother, Wilhelmine."

"Okay. And my great-grandmother is Bertha, Wilhelmine's sister."

"Since we're cousins, I should introduce myself! I'm Brenda Kruger."

"I was calling you 'Marian the Librarian' in my head, so it's nice to have your name. And I'm Zara Vrabel," she said, shaking Brenda's hand.

"I knew of your great-grandmother. But your family lived in Chicago, and as time passed and the elders died, the newer generations lost touch. Still, I thought I knew of everyone on that side of the family, but apparently not," said Brenda.

"I've gone my whole life knowing nothing about any of you." And Zara explained the backstory. "Oh, and I found a name on the internet white pages that matched a name in the family history: Frank Weidner. I had a photo of him as a little boy with my grandmother."

"Oh, my! Uncle Frank! Yes, he lives in the apartment building just down the street and is the only one left from that generation."

"I feel as if I struck gold," said Zara.

"Well, this is a momentous occasion," said Brenda. "Now that I know who you are, give me a few minutes to get the right church records."

Brenda xeroxed about twenty pages of church records, and various newspaper clippings about their shared families. "Now, these records largely pertain to the late nineteenth and early twentieth centuries when our family first immigrated to western Wisconsin," said Brenda.

"Whodathunk I'd meet a family member I never knew in a place I'd never heard of!" said Zara.

"Well, it's an enormous family," said Brenda. "I'm not surprised that you exist, but I am surprised that you—well—came back. You're a city person, so... what impelled you to care about us?"

"That family history document ignited a flame that's consuming my life. There's a sadness—a wistful nostalgia that I can't shake," said Zara. "I'm yearning for people and places I never knew in this life."

"Well, it's not an accident that we've met. I always found that coincidences are like the speed of light. The closer we get to the source of our roots, the faster the frequency of the coincidences becomes. I'm sure it feels disorienting."

"Meeting living people, like you, is slowly making it more tangible."

"I heard the story of your Aunt Martha's death from my grandmother. So tragic."

"Then, you're one of the very few who knows," said Zara.

"I can't believe that you found us. Well, you're attuned to the clarion call of the ancestors," said Brenda.

"You sound like my best friend, Elly," said Zara. "Say. We've been at it for a few hours now, so what time is your lunch? I'd like to treat you to pay you back for all that xeroxing."

"Nonsense! We're family, so let me buy you lunch to welcome you to Falling Brook."

"You're very kind. So is Crabby Bob's serving?" said Zara.

"Oh, yes, let's go there. Crabby Bob is another cousin, by the way," said Brenda. "And, let me call Uncle Frank to see if he wants a sandwich. We can drop it off afterward, and you can meet him, too."

"Whoa! I feel like I'm in Mayberry! No disrespect, but am I related to everyone here?" said Zara.

"Probably. This is a small place, so everyone is related by blood or marriage. It's a tight-knit community, Zara. It's what kept so many of us from leaving since we all support each other in good times and bad," said Brenda.

They sat in the darkened bar and ordered soup and Cokes.

"And an order of biscuits," said Brenda to Jan, the waiter.

"Is she a cousin?" whispered Zara.

Brenda laughed. "No, but she's married to one of our cousins!"

"These biscuits are something else!" said Zara as she savored the rich hard crust, the underlying sweetness of honey, the saltiness of the butter, and the chewiness of the dough. *Yeah, this tastes like home.*

A man's voice bellowed, "Nothing like 'em!" And Zara jerked her head around to see a man, maybe mid-fifties, with salt-and-pepper hair, medium build, and wearing a white shirt, black pants, and a large apron.

"Oh, hi, Bob," said Brenda. "I want to introduce you to a long-lost cousin!" And the formerly taciturn Brenda recounted Zara's backstory to Bob, mentioning that she was a published writer, while Zara scarfed down another biscuit.

"Well, I'll be," said Crabby Bob. "We usually don't get celebrity relatives from the big city visiting our humble village."

Zara understood immediately how Bob earned the "crabby" part of his name and tossed some snark in his direction. "Oh, Crabby Bob, I'm no celebrity—just a coal-miner's granddaughter from Johnstown, Pennsylvania."

Crabby Bob laughed and said, "The Flood City, huh? Well, that's a long distance from there to here."

"In more ways than one, Bob," said Zara.

"LET me give you the names of other people that you're related to. Living people, I mean," said Brenda, who began writing names and phone numbers.

"I actually have to get back to the Cities, Brenda," said Zara, looking at her watch.

"All right then. Let's plan for you to come back. Many people will want to meet you," said Brenda.

"Sounds like a plan, ma'am," said Zara.

"Bob! A roast beef and potatoes for Uncle Frank," said Brenda.

Brenda and Zara walked half a block to a small apartment complex and into the lobby. Zara was shocked that the outer door was open, and that there was no security. They climbed the stairs to the second floor, and Brenda rapped on the door.

An older pleasant-looking man, with curly gray hair, weathered skin, and kind blue eyes, answered. He fit Zara's idea of a farmer.

With a red-and-grey flannel shirt, blue jeans, and cowboy boots, he was an older Marlboro Man. They followed him into a wonderfully appointed studio apartment. It was neat and comfortable, with a leather couch and chair in front of a wide-screen TV. There was a kitchenette and a small dining area, and large windows overlooking the park.

Brenda did her best to explain to Frank who this petite blonde stranger was. While he seemed to be hard of hearing, Frank's face lit up when it finally registered. "You look like one of those Pfeiffer girls!"

And Zara smiled and said, "Thank you."

The sight of me reminded him of days gone by, and he cried while I remained stunned. I was one of the Pfeiffer girls, and I was also changing those I met. This is lifting me out of myself and depositing me into the lives of others. Strangers, yes, but we share blood. What does sharing blood really mean?

They had a brief visit as Frank had a doctor's appointment, and Zara was growing anxious to hit the highway before rush hour.

My relationship with this place and these people is at once tactile and thin. I have a sense of belonging, but it is a different belonging than I felt in Chicago. Hard to explain, and maybe time will reveal more.

"Thanks, Brenda, for being so welcoming. I planned on just looking around. I didn't know I'd be spending the afternoon with new-found family!"

"Don't be a stranger, now. We've just found you, and we'll want to know you better," said Brenda.

As Zara was driving toward downtown Saint Paul, she glanced at her eyes in the rearview mirror. *How can this be? I'm the same person who entered this journey nearly two years ago, but even I don't recognize myself.*

20

SEALED ORDERS

"Excited about the dinner party?" asked Elly.

"Naw," said Zara, "I'm going so I don't get out of practice."

"Good," said Elly, pouring Zara another cup of coffee. "Time to get back into life, even if you don't feel like it."

"Present time isn't all that interesting. I left my heart in 1915 Chicago," said Zara.

"Do it! Just go tonight," said Elly.

"Not in the mood," replied Zara.

"I'm afraid you'll have to bite the bullet," said Elly. "It's rough, trying to integrate everything, but you have to. Don't shut the door on the present."

"You stopped dating eons ago, so why do you care if I do too?"

"Because going on a dating hiatus is completely out of character for you. As for me, well, the more men I dated, the more I realized I preferred cats."

"Yeah," shrugged Zara.

"Don't Syl and Binnie have another single girl for you to meet?" asked Elly.

"Oh, those two goofs mean well, but I'd prefer it if they'd stop matchmaking."

Elly was losing patience. "Try to act normal for three hours or so. It won't hurt you. After that, go dancing again, too. Does the Townhouse still have the Friday nights swing dances?

"I dunno. I heard they cut them out," said Zara.

"Well, if you and Miss-Close-to-Right get along, maybe you can continue the party at the bar," said Elly.

"Oh, Elly!" said Zara.

"Shut up! Now, go out and buy some new hair products. That used to cheer you up. Then, get going and call me with every gory detail on Saturday."

~

THAT EVENING, Zara stared at herself in the full-length mirror.

"Not bad," she said, scrutinizing her look: tight black jeans, Doc Martens high-tops, grey scooped neck top, and black leather jacket.

"Where have we been?" she said to her reflection. "Elly's right. I have to get in the game again."

~

SYL AND BINNIE—ROTUND, aging versions of the Campbell's Soup Kids—were Zara's friends from seminary.

"Here's a sight for sore eyes," said Syl, hugging Zara. Several other people nodded amiably, except Kathy Dean, another seminary classmate. Zara never understood why Kathy had competed with her almost from the time they met. If Zara led church services, Kathy Dean had to do it the following Sunday. If Zara preached, Kathy also followed up with a sermon the next Sunday.

Zara shook her head. "It was like getting pecked to death by ducks," she thought while remembering Kathy Dean's antics.

When they were in school, everywhere she turned, Kathy Dean

was there. If she wasn't watching Zara, Kathy Dean was milking crowds, talking about how hard it was to be gay in the church, and how much everyone owed her.

One Sunday after church, Zara cornered her.

"Stop acting like an oppressed lesbian poster child for the Lutheran Church. Show some courage and self-respect!" said Zara shaking her head. "Lots of secondary gains to be had from playing the victim, huh, Kathy?"

For once, Kathy was speechless and avoided Zara after that exchange.

~

KATHY GRUNTED as Zara walked through the living room, and Zara grunted in reply.

Binnie introduced Zara to the other single woman. Liisa, who towered over Zara by a foot, was from Finland—and Zara loved accents. After developing a neck crick from looking up, Zara convinced the woman to sit on the couch. They made small talk, which Zara found exhausting. Fifteen minutes passed, and Zara was ready to leave. She paused when she noticed tears flooding Liisa's eyes.

"What's wrong?" said Zara.

"Ah, it's..." said Liisa, dabbing her eyes with the tissue Zara handed her. "It's an anniversary. A somber anniversary. My mother and my father were killed in a car accident on this date five years ago, and I miss them so."

Zara took the woman's hand and led her to the kitchen, while the others scattered to give them privacy.

"I'll never see them again," said Liisa. "They're gone forever, and I can't..."

"No!" Zara shouted. "Don't ever think that! They're standing with you now. Your dad his hand on your left shoulder. Your mom is next to him on your right. They wish you'd stop crying long enough to listen—they didn't abandon you. They said you cried about it last week in the hotel when you thought about taking the Xanax and booze. Your mother said to tell you that's no way to meet them. 'Wait for your time,' she said."

Liisa's eyes widened, and she grabbed Zara, digging her nails into her shoulders.

"You couldn't possibly know that!? But it's true. What manner of person are you?"

Zara could not tell if the woman was exhilarated, infuriated, or terrified.

She paused, scarcely believing what she was saying.

"I—uh—I'm so, so sorry. I don't know what came over me! Honest! I didn't mean to say all that! I couldn't stop myself," said Zara.

"Don't apologize, Zara. The night I was in the hotel, I had a lot of the Xanax. I had been, what do you call it, stockpiling it. And the vodka. I wanted to die. I prayed to my parents that night and screamed at them to take away this hole in my heart. Then, I felt a cool breeze come over me and a scent, like my mother's perfume, filled the room. I fell asleep and never touched the drugs or the booze."

"Liisa, I don't know how I know these things, but I do," said Zara. "I recently had a long-dead relative who made contact. She's convinced me that life doesn't end after death. I'm new at this, but I also come from a long line of women who communed as easily with the dead as I'm talking with you now. The departed who love us sometimes go to extreme means to be there when we mess up."

"Yes, yes, I want to believe it," said Liisa.

"Then listen to your parents," said Zara.

"You see them, Zara?" asked Liisa. Zara nodded. "What do you see then? Tell me."

"Well, it's not clear, but there is a very tall man who looks more like you than the short woman at his side," said Zara, staring just beyond Liisa's shoulders. "The woman is hazy but puts her index finger to her mouth as if to say 'hush.'"

"Oh Lord," said Liisa, crying, "That's what she would do when she put us to bed at night when we were little. We'd try to get her to tell one more story, or sing one more song, and she would say 'Hush, hush, time for dreamland.'"

Zara and Liisa talked a while longer.

"Can I see you again, Zara?" whispered Liisa.

"I'll help you if I can, but these impressions don't appear on demand. You've caught me amid figuring this stuff out. And also, I don't want to be misleading you. Y'know—the romantic thing."

"Ja, I understand. I just want to know what you've seen and what you've learned," said Liisa.

"Fine," said Zara, laughing. "I've only spoken about this with my best friend, and I'm sure she'd be grateful if I'd talk with someone else about it once in a while."

∼

"ZARA, you have got to be shittin' me! That woman's probably packing for Helsinki by now!" said Elly, putting bread in the toaster.

"It was weird, El. It was like watching myself in a play, getting fed lines from offstage. Those words that came out of my mouth didn't feel like me, yet I knew they were mine. There was a certainty and confidence in how I told that woman about life after death. And I saw her parents standing behind her!"

"Whoa! My God, Zara," said Elly taking her hand, "You saw her parents? Were they ghosts or solid?"

Zara closed her eyes and took a deep breath. "They were hazy with features fading in and out. They didn't stay the same. Parts of them would come into sharp focus and then blur out."

"So, what did you feel?" said Elly.

"Feel?" said Zara. "Nothing. It was like spotting a deer in the forest and being surprised."

"You mean you weren't scared?" said Elly.

"No. It felt as if I'd done this my whole life. Maybe I have," said Zara.

"What do you mean?" said Elly.

"I don't think this is the first time I've done something like this. I mean randomly with strangers—not family. But I blot it out as soon as it happens," said Zara.

"How exciting! You're a natural!" said Elly.

"Who knew?" said Zara.

"You've tapped into something compelling, Zara. Keep a journal. You need to learn how to focus these talents so you're not all over the place."

"Just because I'm talented at something doesn't mean I want to do it," said Zara. "I don't want to see the dearly departed!"

"Have it your way," said Elly getting two mugs from the cupboard. "But eventually, your gifts are going to ambush you. You're going to have to deal with it!"

"Fine," said Zara, as she watched Elly fill their mugs.

"I don't get you—I will never get you. Why are you still fighting this? Even someone returning from the dead isn't enough to get your attention. Geez! Until the last couple of years or so, you weren't going anyplace," said Elly.

Zara squinted, and she snarled, "Oh, I resent that!"

"On the surface, everything was fine—you were successful, you were doing creative things and all that. But you also seemed perpetually restless and much younger than your years, but not in a complimentary way. I used to call you Peter Pan, and I meant it," said Elly.

"You want me to embrace the talking-to-the-dead thing? Who's going to believe me?" said Zara.

"Ask your new friend from Finland," said Elly.

"But Elly, what a thing to be allied with. So many so-called psychics are charlatans."

"We're back to that again. Look. There are charlatans in every profession—attorneys, physicians, and let us not forget, the clergy. Remember: to those who believe, no proof is necessary—to those who don't, no proof is possible," said Elly.

"How poetic," said Zara.

"It's from the *Song of Bernadette*, but it applies. And, ready or not, you're finally coming into your own. Embrace it."

"One thing at a time. I still have the *Eastland* to contend with," said Zara.

21

THE RETURN OF THE EASTLAND— 2000

Nearly three years had passed since Zara first learned about the lost branches of her maternal ancestors, and the *Eastland* Disaster. But things changed.

Pearl's health and mental state had declined, and she now lived in a care facility. Zara was grateful for the time they'd had, but gratitude alone did not assuage the guilt she felt for not reaching out sooner. Zara prepared herself as much as possible for the inevitable "promotion," which was Pearl's description of death. She hoped Pearl knew her life's work—the family history—was secure in Zara's capable hands.

On the positive side, a newly formed Eastland Society was created in Chicago by those whose families were touched by the disaster. She emailed the website owner, explaining her connection.

Gladys Oleksienko, the daughter of a survivor, and society co-founder, surprised Zara with a phone call.

Gladys said, "We're not wasting any more time! We've contacted the folks organizing the *Titanic* Exhibition at the Museum of Science and Industry and convinced them to host an exhibit for the *Eastland* Disaster. Think of it! We will show the *Eastland* in conjunction with the *Titanic!*"

"Long overdue," said Zara.

"There are a lot of us, Zara. Thanks to the internet, families who were affected by the *Eastland* can find one another. I'm 80 years old, and if I can figure out the internet, anyone can."

"I learned of it just three years ago," said Zara.

"My goodness!" said Gladys. "This has to be quite a journey for you. Still, even if you'd grown up in Chicago, you might not have known about it, because some families never discussed it," said Gladys. "My mother survived but only talked about the details right before she died. When I was a child, I never understood why she'd cry when we wanted to go swimming. She was so nervous and high-strung, and I chalked it up to eccentricity. Then, when I got older, she told me bits and pieces. She was on the deck when the ship tipped over and was in that filthy river for hours. She watched bodies floating past her and never recovered. Poor darling was probably suffering from post-traumatic stress disorder, and there was no help back then. They just carried on and tried to forget."

"How old was your mother when it happened?" said Zara.

"She was just 18," said Gladys.

"My great-aunt was 19," said Zara.

"Sorry, so sorry," said Gladys. "This shouldn't have happened to our families. They knew that ship was trouble—should have been scrapped long before 1915. Now, we descendants live with the aftermath."

Gladys' phrase, *our families*, struck Zara. This was another kind of family, bound by catastrophe, not DNA. A grief so encompassing that it sliced across culture, religion, gender, class, and even time. Yes, these people, too, were her family.

"Even without knowing my great-aunt, I've followed in her foot-steps throughout my life," said Zara.

"I believe it," said Gladys. "Our deceased relatives love and guide us."

"Well, I can't wait to meet you," said Zara. "Trying to cram a life-time of lost family history into a few years has been a wild ride."

"Well, it's like learning a new language. Although, of course, it's easier to learn a language as a child, but not impossible for an adult," said Gladys.

"Never thought of it that way," said Zara.

"It's a language of the soul, of the heart," said Gladys. "I'll see you in July, Zara."

"Good luck in putting everything together."

A WEEK LATER, the invitation arrived in the mail. On Saturday, July 22, 2000, the *Eastland* artifacts would display, along with the touring *Titanic* exhibit, at the Museum of Science and Industry in Hyde Park. The museum, touted as the "largest science center in the Western Hemisphere" was the former Palace of Fine Arts from the 1893 World's Columbian Exposition.

This promised to be an elegant affair with dinner and a program. Descendants of survivors and victims—and maybe a couple of remaining survivors—would also attend.

"It looks as if the *Eastland* is finally hitting the big time," said Elly. "First a website, a memorial society, and now—drumroll—an exhibit juxtaposed with the *Titanic*. That's good, right? Plus, you'll meet other families and who knows what stories they have."

"There was next to nothing when I started, and now it's exploding," said Zara. "I loved talking with someone else with a similar story. The story is finally being dredged from the Chicago River, and it will take its rightful place in history. That's all I thought I wanted for it," said Zara.

"Well," said Elly. "This is just thrilling, so why are you so mopey? This event could change your life."

Zara rolled her eyes. "Change my life? Again? My life is unrecognizable at this point. The former life, the former me, no longer exists. I'm stranded between worlds, and worry that what happened to the *Titanic* will happen to the *Eastland*. It feels fragile, and I loathe to think of opportunists climbing out of the woodwork, trying to make a buck off it."

"Oh, just cool your jets and promise not to bring this up again—it's getting old, Zara! Opportunists have been making money off tragedies since time immemorial. Hell, some create the tragedies so they can profit. Forget them! Focus on what you need to do, and stop fussing over things that haven't happened," said Elly.

"I can't help it," said Zara.

Elly stared at Zara. "Your life was never completely your own. Maybe that's the point—you're carrying other lives and other responsibilities besides your own. Maybe we all are, but your situation is truly over the top."

Zara's eyes widened. "Yeah," she whispered, "I accept it, and, sadly, this tragedy is the only palpable way I can connect to Martha."

"I get that," said Elly. "This feels like the grand finale, and we owe this to her. It's been good for me, too. Traveling to Chicago, as often as we have, has forced me to deal with stuff from my past. I'm sure glad Martha's had me riding shotgun."

"I gotta see what they have of the *Eastland*," said Zara. "See what Martha saw. And, whether I'm ready or not, it's time to meet others. Maybe their ancestor knew mine—you never know."

"You're really different now—in a good way. Stronger. You're actually more sure of yourself. Not so much self-doubt. This event, too, is going to be a turning point." said Elly.

"This is strange. I'm going as one of those Pfeiffer girls—the only representative of my family. I never thought my family would want me representing them in anything," said Zara.

"Your dead relative seems to think you're more than worthy. So, I'd listen to her," said Elly.

∽

ELLY AND ZARA settled into their seats on the quick flight from Minneapolis-Saint Paul to Chicago. Elly buried her nose in the *Chicago Tribune*, while Zara wrote in her journal:

We are not here for *Titanic* fever! Instead, there's another exhibit of a "lesser shipwreck," as one paper called it, inside that makeshift wall I must witness.

After landing in Midway, they deplaned, picked up the rental car, and pulled out a map to the Museum of Science and Industry. Again, Zara made record time, navigating the streets of Chicago.

"I gotta hand it to you, Zara, you're almost a native Chicagoan now. I can't believe that you, with your lousy sense of direction, now zip through the streets of the Windy City!" said Elly.

"Well, it's easy once you get your Chicago sea legs, so to speak," she said, steering around some broken glass.

"Say, did Gladys give you a final headcount?"

"I guess there will be about 300 attending. Geez, this is so emotional. D'you suppose any of them are visited by any dead relatives?" said Zara.

"I bet you're not the only one but, hold on—there's the sign for Garfield Blvd. Get off here." And they pulled into the underground parking.

Zara and Elly took the elevator to the Great Exhibit Hall.

"This is so cool! I haven't been here since I was a kid," said Elly. "I forgot how large it was."

"You have the tickets?" said Zara.

"Here in my purse," said Elly. "Oh, my. Look at this!"

Standing in the Great Exhibit Hall was like walking into Valhalla. They were hemmed in by colossal screens running newsreels of the *Titanic*. Yet, for all the people milling about, it was eerily silent, except for the rumblings of a bass drum in the background.

"This is... it cuts right to the heart, doesn't it?"

"It does. Although I've resented the inordinate amount of attention the *Titanic* keeps getting, fact is, death is death. But, can we get away from this? It's too much," said Zara.

"Let's explore," said Elly. "The exhibit doesn't open for another 20 minutes, so we have time."

"I hate waiting. I've waited long enough and must see those artifacts of that 'lesser shipwreck.' Damn! That ship cost our family so much!" As Zara paced, her heels sounded as if they were transmitting Morse code against the hard tile.

"Okay, okay," said Elly. "It will feel better after today, so hang in there."

"Hey, look over there," said Zara, pointing to a display of horse-drawn and electric streetcars.

"Come on!" said Elly. She and Zara hopped onto an electric trolley.

"People must have been a lot smaller in the early 1900s. I can barely squeeze my backside in here," said Elly.

"It's tiny, all right," said Zara, readjusting herself on the wooden seat. "I wonder what kind Martha rode on the way to the picnic?"

"Ask her!" said Elly.

They jumped off the streetcar and continued walking.

"Omigod," said Elly, staring at the kiosk directory. "I forgot about the Street of Yesteryear. We gotta see this—they constructed a street from turn-of-the-century Chicago—Martha's time!"

They raced down the stairs.

"Look at this," said Zara, surveying the exhibit.

They strolled over cobblestones and wooden sidewalks, gazing inside shoe stores, hat stores, restaurants, a post office, and an apothecary.

"I can't believe it," said Zara. "It's like stepping inside an old painting."

"I love the dress styles! To live in a time where skeletal doesn't define beauty would be paradise," said Elly, studying the mannequins in a dress shop window.

"Walgreens? They had Walgreens back then?" said Zara.

"Oh, wait. There's a movie house," said Elly, pointing to a tiny room with a screen and benches.

"A Nickelodeon!" said Zara, who began mangling the lyrics to an old song about a Nickelodeon

"That's an awful imitation of Teresa Brewer!" said Elly.

Elly and Zara sat on hard wooden benches, watching a Buster Keaton short.

"Would she have seen this movie?" said Elly.

"No, I think Buster Keaton came a few years after her death. She would have seen Lillian Gish, Charlie Chaplin, or Mary Pickford."

"How about Fay Wray?" said Elly.

"Nope, Fay wasn't born until 1904 and made her early films in the 1920s," said Zara.

"I was joking about Fay Wray! How in the hell do you know about silent films that were made over half a century before you were born?" said Elly.

"Huh?" said Zara, leaning backward and catching herself.

"Watch it," said Elly, pushing her forward. "No backs on these benches."

"I loved silent movies since I was a little kid," said Zara.

"Where'd you see them? They didn't show them on TV when we were kids, did they?" said Elly.

"A few. The 'Our Gang' shorts and Charlie Chaplin. I learned about them from my mom's 1946 *World Book Encyclopedia*, volume *M* —it had photos of Mary Pickford, John Bunny, and William S. Hart. I'd look at them for hours. Strange, huh?" said Zara.

"No. Completely normal—for someone born in 1895! It's as if Martha picked up where she left off when you were born. That could explain your ship phobia, too," said Elly.

"Am I Martha reincarnated?" said Zara.

"You share blood and the same ancestors," said Elly. "What do you think?"

"I'm the next chapter—a continuation of those who've gone before me."

"You're intertwined via those beautiful DNA strands. Now, lighten up and have fun! This is a perfect place for Martha's past to catch up to your present," said Elly.

"Elly, let's go before I demolecularize and become a permanent part of this exhibit."

Elly kept walking and noticed Zara stayed behind.

"Hey, kiddo. What are you doing?" said Elly, who returned to where Zara stood.

"Lots of streets like this that I once walked down. I recognize this from before," said Zara.

Elly froze, then looked at Zara's eyes. Her eyes—without expression or light. Vacant and yet gazing. A chill ran down Elly's spine, and she thought, *get her out of here.*

"Let's go. I'm thirsty, and there's a little cafeteria over here," said Elly, gently taking Zara's arm. "You all right, hon? You seem not quite here."

"I'm fine," Zara whispered.

"Want a Coke?" said Elly. "My treat! Have a seat, and I'll be right back."

The cafeteria couldn't have been tackier, with plastic chairs, a sticky floor, and hordes roaming about. A severe, but needed, contrast. "Unchained Melody" began playing as Zara leaned back and squinted at the fluorescent lighting.

Elly quickly returned with drinks, heard the music, and smiled. "Well, kiddo, even Muzak is sending you cues today."

"I guess so," said Zara, laughing. "Thanks. I am thirsty as hell!"

"How are you? It seemed you were floating away back there," said Elly.

"That was damn weird. I felt as if I was in two places at once," said Zara, pointing to the street. "Umm, you're the one I'm worried about. You look kind of pasty green."

Elly chuckled. "Oh, I'm fine. It's just that nearly every *Twilight Zone* I ever saw passed before my eyes when we were back there."

Zara, Elly, and a cast of hundreds lined up for the *Titanic* and *Eastland* exhibit opening. Everyone streamed past Elly and Zara to ogle the *Titanic* artifacts. The first artifact to greet them was a tarnished brass bell that was sounded when *RMS Titanic* was heading toward the iceberg.

"That sets the mood," said Zara.

"No kidding. It's as if we're walking into a crypt."

"Oh, we are," said Zara.

"Is this the actual bell?"

"I think so. And there's a bit of controversy. A company bought exclusive rights to salvage the wreck and sell or rent the artifacts. Not sure how that works."

They continued walking through the various reconstructed rooms.

"Holy smokes," said Elly. "Talk about the gilded age coming the life. This is like walking through Glensheen Mansion or the J.J. Hill house."

"I don't think we creatures of the twenty-first century understand opulence the way they did back then!"

"What do you think of it?"

"Controversy aside, it's very respectful. I like the progression from bright and cheery to dark and foreboding. It's unnerving, seeing the actual hull fragments," said Zara.

"Believe it or not, I'm getting a bit emotional about it."

"We're almost done," said Zara, and she bolted ahead, nearly climbing over the *Titanic* people.

At the end of the exhibit is the reason she was here, her destiny.

She saw a small sign that read *Exhibit: The Eastland: Chicago's Titanic* and raced toward it.

Leaning against the pillar, Zara sighed.

It's just you and me again. She gazed at a life preserver with the *SS Eastland* insignia. *Why didn't you find your way to it?* Deck chairs, photos, newspaper clippings, boarding tickets, programs—things that were aboard that cursed vessel. *Did you see them? Touch them?*

"Well, I never heard of this," said an older woman to her friend, "And I've lived here all my life. Did you ever hear of this?"

The friend said, "No."

Zara wanted to grab and throttle the woman, but she shook her head, wondering what on earth, or in heaven, could make Chicago and the world forget this day.

"What is that?" said Elly.

"Oh, it's an Uncle Sam costume, worn by one of the survivors—a kid who wanted to march in a parade at the picnic. He was wearing it when he boarded. He stood out in the costume and was one of the first people plucked from the water."

"Uh oh. The *Titanic* helped kill the *Eastland*!"

"What?"

"That video talked about the LaFollette Seaman's Act, which passed after the *Titanic*. Ships were required to have enough lifeboats for each passenger, and that's what helped make the *Eastland* a death trap. Take a look."

They walked over to a kiosk running an educational video.

"This was a time where building steamers were very competitive. The *Eastland* was dubbed the 'Speed Queen of the Lakes'. Even back then, many near-accidents and noticeable listing problems led many to speculate about the ship's safety."

"Now I remember that from when I first started researching."

They continued, looking at deck chairs, a cane, and a diving suit.

"Not as posh as the *Titanic*,"

"Doesn't need to be. This has something the *Titanic* never will."

"What's that?"

"Look at the gallery of photos taken by Jun Fujita. He was there to photograph the picnic and ended up as the chief witness to the tragedy."

"Despite the subject, these are gorgeous. Can you imagine, showing up at a job site thinking that you're photographing a corporate event, and this happens."

"Now that's professionalism!"

"I overheard someone talking about the Chicago River being cursed!"

"What the heck?"

"Yeah. Did you know they reversed the Chicago River in 1900 to make it flow toward the Mississippi? I guess they wanted to redirect the sewage flow."

"Oh, the places my mind could go with that. But not today."

THE DINNER, held in a banquet room, was a lovely event with speeches, music, and even a play about an *Eastland* victim. Then the names were called out, not all 844 of them, but the names of those represented by family.

"Martha Elizabeth Pfeiffer, represented by her grand-niece, Zara Vrabel," said the young emcee.

Zara stood while the audience applauded.

After the dinner, Gladys Oleksienko made her way to Zara and Elly's table. Gladys, a retired teacher, was tall, well-dressed, and neatly coiffed. She embraced Zara and whispered, "Zara, I feel I've known you my whole life!"

"I feel the same, Gladys," said Zara. "Maybe my aunt knew your mother."

"And your friend came with you!" said Gladys.

Elly said, "I wouldn't have missed this for the world."

Zara smiled and said, "Elly is my best friend, and the most patient human in the world!"

The women circled the exhibit again. The museum was closed to the public by then, and event attendees walked, talked, and stood silent as they stared.

"Well Zara," said Gladys. "I don't remember the name, Pfeiffer. But what matters is that you and I have met!"

Gladys recounted stories of other family members, and neighbors whose lives spiraled out of control after the *Eastland* tragedy.

"My uncles who survived it both felt guilty for the rest of their lives," said Gladys. "They both died from alcoholism, but I say they died from the *Eastland*. Zara—I want you to meet someone."

Gladys led Zara across the floor toward an older woman.

"This is Lily Jesenick," said Gladys. "She was four years old when it happened. Lily. This is Zara Vrabel. She lost someone on the ship."

Zara shook her hand, and Lily, nearly 90 years old, looked into Zara's eyes and smiled. Just five feet tall, Lily's face was barely lined. She wore her straight grey-black hair in a quasi-Louise Brooks bob, and her tattered yellow and black paisley print dress was probably a relic from the Summer of Love.

"You remember the day, Lily?" asked Zara.

The waiflike woman's blue eyes brightened, and she continued clutching Zara's hand. "I forget things that happened last week, but I never forget that day. My dad died in the water, along with my two sisters. My mother and I held onto a crate until we were rescued. Bodies floating by—you never forget."

"Lily, do you remember anyone else on the ship?" said Zara.

"Our cousins and neighbors were there. They survived. What about you? Who did you lose?" said Lily.

"My Great-Aunt Martha Pfeiffer. She was nineteen."

"Nineteen. Most of the people were young like that. Do you still live in Chicago?"

"No, I've never lived here. My great-grandparents lived here, and my grandmother worked for Western Electric in Cicero."

"What about your great-aunt?" said Lily.

"She didn't work for Western Electric. My grandmother was pregnant and gave her sister her tickets."

"Oh, my," said Lily, touching her heart with her free hand. "So, your grandmother felt responsible."

"I don't know," said Zara. "My grandmother died when my mother was three."

"How did you learn about the *Eastland*?" said Lily.

Zara explained the story.

"Dear, dear. Be patient, all right? This will take some getting used to," said Lily. "The people who died that day don't always rest in peace."

Zara didn't want to appear too anxious. "What do you mean, Lily?"

"Well, it took a while for me to realize that my dad and sisters were dead, because I saw them every day for at least a few years afterward. Mother finally got so angry that she'd scream and cry and told me they were dead and that I couldn't possibly see them. Well, I didn't understand what dead even meant, but I guess, being a good girl, I obeyed my mother and stopped seeing them. But you know what?"

"Tell me, Lily," said Zara, leaning closer to the woman's face.

"I see them all now. My mom, dad, and sisters—and not just in my dreams, but in my apartment. They're there now. You don't think I'm a crazy old lady, do you?" said Lily.

"Lily, I believe you because I've had almost the same experiences," said Zara. "I haven't told too many people about it."

"Me neither because I'm afraid my son's wife will lock me up. My son died a few years back, and his widow is not very nice," said Lily.

"Well, Lily, if you're crazy, then I am, too!"

Lily laughed, "I'm so glad that I met you, Zara, and that you told me about your Martha."

"Lily, you got closer to her than anyone else in this room," said Zara. "And I'm honored to meet you."

"Keep talking to your Martha now. She must love you so much to travel alongside you," said Lily.

"That's so kind, Lily," said Zara. "I'll take your words with me for the rest of my life."

"Goodbye, Zara," said Lily, hugging Zara. "I'm pleased to call you my friend."

As they exited the Museum, Elly said, "Gladys was great, wasn't she? You ought to keep in contact with her. And Lily! Some connection. You and an actual survivor. And she told you to keep talking to Martha!"

"As if I have any choice," laughed Zara. "Elly. I also think that this is it. This is the last thing I'll be doing with the *Eastland* for a while."

"Why do you think that?" said Elly.

"I've accomplished all I wanted—and then some. It's the apotheosis of this adventure, I guess. So, I'm stopping it in an interesting place—to quote Julia Cameron. I'll know when to pick it up again," said Zara.

"You know what comes to mind? 'Miracles undo the past in the present and thus release the future,'" said Elly. "It's from *A Course in Miracles*. Remember when I studied that?"

"Oh, I tried to forget that. I swear the writer of that thing was on something, but I almost understand it," said Zara.

"But it's what you've done to the event now with the attention you've given to it. You stopped your own life and let her in," said Elly.

"I want to go to the disaster site again," said Zara.

They drove and parked the car just off Clark Street, facing the Reid Murdoch Building.

"You've accomplished something monumental," said Elly.

"It doesn't feel that way."

"Oh, but you did. You learned to talk to the dead—and listen to them. No small feat, that's for sure."

Staring at the slivered moon's pale reflection against the dark of the Chicago River in Zara's face, Elly noticed her pale skin took on shades of blue, and her eyes looked like jade embedded in a statue. Elly shivered.

"Martha?" said Elly quietly, taking Zara's hand.

Zara turned to her friend and said, "Did you know what you just called me?"

"My God, Zara, I understand. She lives! She's here! You're the conduit."

"Elly, I don't know."

"I guess this is one of the greatest love stories I've ever seen, and I didn't know it until just now."

"I do love her. Hmm. In the beginning, I wanted it to be over. It was so unnerving. I wanted a neat little Hollywood ending that explains everything," said Zara.

"Since when do families have neat little Hollywood endings?" said Elly. "With Pearl not doing well, it's time that you step up and become the family historian."

"Well, Pearl's a writer. I'm a writer. Genealogy seems like a natural segue. And my investigation skills are on point!"

"Now you're talking! And you and I have things to do—just like the good old days, but better. Gosh. I wish we had two flowers to place in the river again," Elly said.

"Oh, we have one flower in that river," said Zara. As they walked away, Zara turned for a last look. Then, out of the corner of her eye, she saw something on the river and Zara blew a kiss.

Elly never looked back but said, "Come on, kid. I'll drive back to the hotel so you can have a good cry."

NOTES

2. Annie's Granddaughter

1. Gibran, Kahlil. "On Children." *The Prophet*, 1923.

5. Living in the Past

1. Zett, Natalie. "On the Eastland," *Park Bugle*, 1998. http://www.parkbugle.org
2. Hilton, George W. Eastland: Legacy of the Titanic. Stanford University Press. 2005.

6. Sketching an Un-lived Life

1. Dickinson, Emily. "Death Sets a Thing Significant." 101 Great American Poems: An Anthology, Dover Pub., Mineola, NY, 1998.
2. Celine Dion. "To Love You More." Celine Dion All the Way: A Decade of Song, Columbia/Legacy.
3. Bronte, Emily. "Plead for Me." *Poets of the English Language*, Viking Press, New York, 1950.

8. Visiting Pearl

1. "We are Family," Sister Sledge, Rhino.
2. Honda, Ishiro, director, *Mothra*. Toho studio, 1961.
3. John 4:10 (NIV)
4. Sandburg, Carl. "What Caused the Eastland Disaster?" SocialistWorker.org, https://socialistworker.org/2015/07/24what-caused-the-eastland-disaster.
5. Sandburg, Carl. *The Eastland*. 1878-1967. https://www.ideals.illinois.edu/bitstream/handle2142/30232/sand-east.pdf?sequence=2.

9. Tracing her Steps

1. "The Trouble with Angels." Released by Columbia Pictures, 1966.

18. Just Passing Through

1. The Book of Common Prayer, 1662. *Morning Prayer* General Confession

ACKNOWLEDGMENTS

To those who walked with me on this journey, I am grateful forever:

- **Pat Benincasa.** The best life partner anyone could hope for.
- **Lisa Bostnar.** My blood and brilliant and compassionate star.
- **Jo Ellen Maurer.** My lifelong friend and Chicagoan who led me into the past.
- **Pearl Donovan Cerny.** My aunt and the keeper of the stories.
- **Martha Elizabeth Pfeiffer.** My great-aunt and guiding light. Forever 19 years old.
- **Anna Ottilie Pfeiffer Donovan Ott.** My maternal grandmother.
- **Betty Ann Helen Ott Zett.** My mother.
- **Ted Wachholz.** Along with his family, Ted created The Eastland Disaster Historical Society and has kept the story of the Eastland alive since 1998.
- **Carl Sandburg.** Thank you for "looking 'em over," sizing 'em up, and calling 'em out.

∼

For any inquiries regarding this book, please email: zett@becominganancestor.com

ABOUT THE AUTHOR

Who am I? Does it really matter? No. But here goes:

In second grade, I wrote my first story, "The Mummy's Hand." This launched my unofficial writing career and prompted my teacher to send me to the school psychologist.

Many years later, a magazine accepted my article about my misadventures in an alternative religious community. A career was born! Also, that alternative community provided a life lesson: no experience is useless, since it can always serve as an example of what not to do.

After returning to civilization, I'd adjusted enough to the so-called real world to acquire a couple of degrees, hold down sundry corporate jobs, and maintain a freelance writing and teaching career. I nearly forgot—I'm also a family historian/genealogist.

I'm a proud granddaughter of eccentric, talented, slightly tortured, and always magical Eastern European immigrants. Each day, I thank my ancestors for being everything—except normal.

Since the areas my grandparents immigrated from no longer exist, I can say—along with fellow Carpatho-Rusyn, Andy Warhol—I am from nowhere. In this incarnation, though, I was born in beautiful Johnstown, PA, and am now based in Minneapolis-Saint Paul.

So thanks for buying my book, since I owe people money. And, if you want to see the photos and other stories behind this work of historical fiction, www.flowerintheriver.com

Made in the USA
Monee, IL
05 January 2022

87989942R00135